Structured COBOL Programming

J M Triance

PUBLISHED BY NCC PUBLICATIONS

British Library Cataloguing in Publication Data

Triance, J. M.
  Structured COBOL programming.
  1. COBOL (Computer program language)
  2. Structured programming
  I. Title
  001.64'2   QA76.73.C25

  ISBN 0-85012-421-2

First published in 1984 by:

NCC Publications, The National Computing Centre Limited, Oxford Road, Manchester M1 7ED

Typeset in 11pt Press Roman by Focal Design Studios Limited, New Mills, Stockport, Cheshire

Printed in England by Hobbs the Printers of Southampton.

ISBN 0-85012-421-2

How To Use
This Book

Each chapter takes one topic and explains the concepts and introduces the COBOL features which are relevant to that topic. A quiz is provided at the end of the chapter to allow you to check your knowledge of the material presented in the chapter. It also guides you towards some of the relevant reference material in the *Structured COBOL Reference Summary*. Finally, after the quiz, some of the less important features of COBOL are introduced. These are separated from the other features to give you the opportunity to omit them if you wish to study COBOL in somewhat less depth.

It is anticipated that readers will read the chapters in order, starting with Chapter 1. After Chapter 9 however, it is possible to alter the sequence in which chapters are read, providing that Chapter 12 is read before Chapter 13.

Acknowledgements

THE BOOK

The course on which the book is based was developed jointly with the National Computing Centre and has been run in the Computation Department at UMIST. My thanks are due to the staff at the NCC and the staff and students at UMIST who made such a valuable contribution to these two activities.

In particular, many of the ideas and much of the material result from the inspired contribution of David Redclift.

THE LANGUAGE

COBOL is an industry language and is not the property of any company or group of companies, or of any organisation or group of organisations.

No warranty, expressed or implied, is made by any contributor or by the CODASYL Programming Language Committee as to the accuracy and functioning of the programming system and language. Moreover, no responsibility is assumed by any contributor, or by the committee, in connection therewith.

The authors and copyright holders of the copyrighted material used herein

> FLOW-MATIC (trademark of Sperry Rand Corporation), Programming for the UNIVAC® I and II, Data Automation Systems copyrighted 1958, 1959, by Sperry Rand Corporation; IBM Commercial Translator Form No. F 28-8013, copyrighted 1959 by IBM; FACT, DSI 27A5260-2760, copyrighted 1960 by Minneapolis-Honeywell

have specifically authorised the use of this material in whole or in part, in the COBOL specifications. Such authorisation extends to the reproduction and use of COBOL specifications in programming manuals or similar publications.

Contents

1 Introduction

1.1 A TYPICAL OFFICE

To understand what COBOL is all about we will start in a typical office. The office we will look at (see figure 1.1) is an electricity company and a clerk is sitting behind a desk with a pile of meter readings in the in-tray and a pile of blank invoices in front of her.

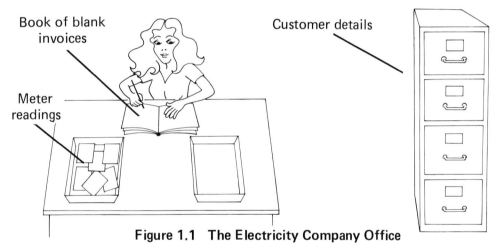

Book of blank invoices

Customer details

Meter readings

Figure 1.1   The Electricity Company Office

The clerk's job is to produce bills for the customers. To do this she takes the meter readings one at a time (an example of a meter reading is shown in figure 1.2).

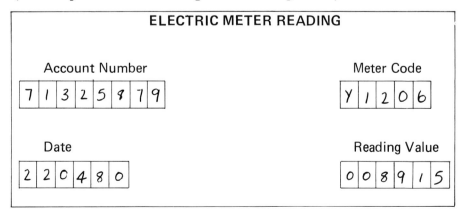

ELECTRIC METER READING

Account Number

| 7 | 1 | 3 | 2 | 5 | 9 | 7 | 9 |

Meter Code

| Y | 1 | 2 | 0 | 6 |

Date

| 2 | 2 | 0 | 4 | 8 | 0 |

Reading Value

| 0 | 0 | 8 | 9 | 1 | 5 |

Figure 1.2   A Meter Reading

1

The account number on the meter reading form is used to find the details of the customer in the filing cabinet. The clerk then takes a blank invoice and produces a bill for the customer (see figure 1.3). The information on the bill comes from a variety of sources: some comes from the meter reading form (eg date of reading and the present reading value), some comes from the customer details record (the previous reading and the customer's name and address), some comes from the clerk's memory (the pence per unit and date), and finally some is calculated by the clerk (the units used and the amount). The completed bill is placed in the out tray ready for posting to the customer and the clerk starts work on the next reading.

Voltohms Electricity Company	INVOICE		
To: Mr. R. J. Thompsons, 16 Swallows Way, Ipchester, Bucks.			

METER READINGS		UNITS USED	PENCE PER UNIT	AMOUNT £
PRESENT	PREVIOUS			
008915	008104	811	4	32.44

ACCOUNT NO	DATE OF READING	INVOICE DATE	TOTAL NOW DUE
71325879	22/04/80	1/5/80	£ 32.44

Figure 1.3 An Electricity Bill

This is the sort of job that can be done by a computer, in fact your electricity bill is almost certainly produced by a computer. The meter readings would be typed in (or perhaps read by an optical character reader) and the bills would be printed on a line printer. The customer details would most likely be stored on a disk for ease of reference and updating. In computing terminology the collection of meter readings is known as a *file* with each meter reading being a *record* in the file. Likewise we have a file of invoices, with each invoice being a record, and a customer details file made up of customer details records.

On a computer, the job of transferring the information (or data) from the meter reading record and the customer details record to the invoice record is done by a computer program. This program is mainly concerned with 'data processing' — reading files, transferring data from one record to another and creating new files — the calculations performed are very simple. Most programs of this type are written in COBOL.

1.2 BACKGROUND TO COBOL

COBOL was created in the United States in 1959 by a group of computer manufacturers and users who wished to create a language for data processing applications. The name COBOL stands for COmmon Business Oriented Language. It is *business oriented* in the sense that most data processing takes place in the business world — banks, insurance, manufacturing, public utilities, and so on. The word *common* refers to the design aim of making COBOL a language which is common to all computers intended for business applications.

COBOL is in fact available on all such machines with few, if any, exceptions. To help ensure consistency between these many implementations of COBOL the American National Standards Institute periodically publishes a COBOL Standard. This book teaches COBOL as specified by the 1974 Standard — ANS 74 COBOL — supplemented by the Structured Programming features of ANS 8X COBOL which is scheduled to supercede it.

1.3 A SIMPLE PROBLEM

By the time you get to the end of the book you will be able to write programs for producing electricity bills like the ones we saw earlier, and indeed for doing much more difficult tasks. For our first program, however, we will keep things extremely simple. We will take the task of producing a list of the meters which have been read — showing only the Meter Code, and the day and month of the reading (see figure 1.4). This list would be produced by the clerk taking the meter readings (figure 1.2) one at a time and copying across the relevant details onto the next line of the list.

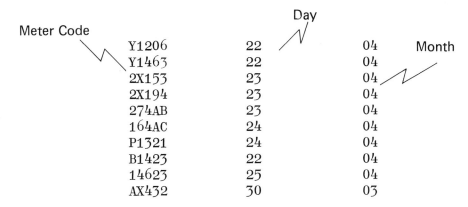

Figure 1.4   List of Meters Read

This list is not completely satisfactory (eg there is no heading to say what the list contains) but remember we want our first problem to be extremely simple. In the next three chapters we will see how to write a COBOL program to produce this list and then in the fifth chapter we will make some improvements to the list and amend our program to produce this improved list.

1.4 COBOL PROGRAM STRUCTURE

In the remainder of this chapter we will look at the structure of COBOL programs and we will write the first part of our first program.

Every COBOL program consists of four divisions — the Identification Division, the Environment Division, the Data Division and the Procedure Division — in that order. Each division begins with a division header — IDENTIFICATION DIVISION, etc. The headers and functions of each division are as follows:

IDENTIFICATION DIVISION

This division contains information which helps to identify the program such as the program-name, the name of the author, the installation, date written and a brief description of the function of the program. Apart from the program-name, the rest of the information is provided solely for the benefit of anyone who reads the program — not for the computer.

ENVIRONMENT DIVISION

This division is used to specify the computers used to compile and run the program. It is also used to specify any other information, particularly relating to files, which is dependent on the type of computer used.

DATA DIVISION

This division describes all the data which is processed by the program whether it is transferred in and out of the computer by means of the files or is used for temporary storage within the computer.

PROCEDURE DIVISION

This division contains the instructions which tell the computer what to do in order to achieve the required results. There are instructions for transferring data between files and the computer's central store, for moving data within the store, for doing arithmetic and for many other tasks.

1.5 THE IDENTIFICATION DIVISION

Figure 1.5 contains an Identification Division for our sample program.

```
IDENTIFICATION DIVISION.
PROGRAM-ID. LIST-METER-RDGS-PROGRAM .
*Author.
*    J. M. TRIANCE.
*Function.
*    This program reads a file of meter readings
*    and lists the meter code, day and month of
*    each of them
```

Figure 1.5 Sample Identification Division

The first entry in the Division is the heading PROGRAM-ID which is followed by the name of the program. I have chosen LIST-METER-RDGS-PROGRAM. Standard COBOL allows any 30 character name to be used but some compilers restrict the user to shorter names. Many installations place further restrictions on the names to ensure that no two programs have the same name or to ensure that related programs have similar names.

After these first two lines, the rest of the Identification Division is optional. It is however good practice to indicate the name of the program's author and to describe the function of the program. This can be done with comment lines such as those used in the example — the lines beginning with the asterisks. These are discussed in the next chapter.

You will notice that the headings, on the first two lines, are followed by full stops as is the entry on the second line. All these full stops are obligatory and each must be followed by a space.

1.6   THE ENVIRONMENT DIVISION

The Environment Division is made up of two Sections. In this chapter we will be looking at the first one — the Configuration Section — which is used to specify the computers used. Figure 1.6 shows the Configuration Section for our sample program.

```
070  ENVIRONMENT DIVISION.
080  CONFIGURATION SECTION.
090  SOURCE-COMPUTER. ANS-2000.
100  OBJECT-COMPUTER. ANS-2000.
```

Figure 1.6   Sample Configuration Section

The Configuration Section starts with the heading CONFIGURATION SECTION and contains two paragraphs — the Source Computer paragraph and the Object Computer paragraph. The first paragraph starts with the heading SOURCE-COMPUTER followed by the name of the computer on which the program is to be compiled. The second paragraph starts with the heading OBJECT-COMPUTER which is followed by the name of the computer on which the program is to run. In this case a fictional computer name, ANS-2000, has been specified since I do not wish to show any bias. However, you will use the names specified by the compiler supplier such as IBM-4341 or VAX-11. In most cases the same computer name will appear in both paragraphs.

Note again the use of full stops after every heading and at the end of each paragraph.

1.7   SUMMARY

We have looked at the overall structure of the COBOL program and in more detail at the first part of it. The headings and entries we have covered are as follows

```
IDENTIFICATION DIVISION.

PROGRAM-ID.  program-name.

*comment-line
     .
     .
     .
ENVIRONMENT DIVISION.

CONFIGURATION SECTION.

SOURCE-COMPUTER.    computer-name.

OBJECT-COMPUTER.    computer-name.

DATA DIVISION.

PROCEDURE DIVISION.
```

QUIZ

Some of these questions can be answered from what you have already learnt. For others you will need to refer to the *Structured COBOL Reference Summary* (NCC, 1984).

1.   Write down the four COBOL divisions in the correct order.

2.   List the errors in the following code

```
    IDENTIFICATION DIVISION.
  *INSTALLATION.  D W H HENRY & SONS
   ENVIROMENT DIVISION.
   CONFIGURATION-SECTION.
   OBJECT-COMPUTER.ANS-2000.
   SOURCE COMPUTER.  ANS-2000.
```

Answers are in Appendix 1.

2 COBOL Language Structure

COBOL is based on the English language. Just as we have to learn rules of grammar before we can write an essay, so also must we learn the rules of construction of COBOL before we can write programs. Fortunately, the rules for COBOL are simpler than they are for English and there are a lot fewer of them.

COBOL has sections (you have already seen the Configuration Section in the Environment Division). It also has paragraphs, sentences, statements, clauses and words. In this chapter we will look at words and how they can be used to construct clauses and statements.

For example, here is a typical COBOL statement:

        ADD 1 TO READING-COUNT.

It consists of three words — ADD, TO and READING-COUNT; and a literal — 1. The first two words ADD and TO have a special meaning in COBOL and can only be used in accordance with the COBOL rules for ADD and TO. These words which have a special meaning are known as *reserved words*. READING-COUNT on the other hand is a name invented by the programmer to represent a particular item of data. We shall be looking at the rules for this type of word and for literals shortly.

In our typical statement you will also notice that we have some spaces and a full stop. The spaces are used as in English to separate words and the full stop as we shall see later is used to terminate COBOL sentences.

2.1 COBOL CHARACTERS

Before we learn about sentences, statements and words we must first see what characters we can use to construct them.

The full set of COBOL characters is shown in figure 2.1. We have already used some letters, a digit, the space and the full stop in our sample statement. The other characters will be introduced as they are needed but you will probably be able to guess the meaning of some of them. Note that some compilers only permit the use of capital letters.

7

Letters:

A B C . . . . Z

Digits:

0 1 2 9

Special Characters:

	space (or blank)
+	plus sign
−	minus sign and hyphen
*	asterisk
/	forward oblique (or stroke or virgule or slash)
=	equal sign
£	currency sign
,	comma
;	semicolon
.	full stop (or period) and decimal point
"	quotation marks
(	left parenthesis (or open bracket)
)	right parenthesis (or close bracket)
>	greater than sign
<	less than sign

Figure 2.1 COBOL Character Set

2.2 COBOL NAMES

Some of the COBOL characters will be used individually but we will more frequently combine them to make up words. We have already seen some of these words. ADD, TO, (and in the previous session) IDENTIFICATION, DIVISION and PROGRAM-ID are all examples of words with a special meaning in the COBOL language – known as reserved words. A full list of these appears in the *Reference Summary* and the meaning of each word will be explained when we come to use it.

The other main type of word is the COBOL name. These are names invented by the programmer to refer to items of data (known as *data-names*), files known as (*file-names*) and various other entities. When devising these names you must follow these rules

1. Use the characters A to Z, 0 to 9 and hyphen

2. Do not use the hyphen as the first or last character

3. Limit the name to a maximum of 30 characters

4. Do not use a reserved word

5. Use at least one letter

Thus some examples of valid names are

ABCDEFGHIJKLMNOPQRSTUVWXYZ1234

LINE-2

A---B

A

Although these names are all acceptable to the COBOL compiler, they are not very good names because, with the possible exception of LINE-2, they do not convey much meaning. You should always choose a name which describes the purpose for which it is being used. This makes the programs easier to read. Thus, in a program that processes meter readings, READING-COUNT is chosen to represent a data item which contains a count of the number of readings.

The following names all convey some meaning:

HEADING

END

OCCURS

COUNT

DATE

As such, you might wish to use them for names. Unfortunately, you can't because they are all reserved words. If in doubt you should consult the list of reserved words before choosing a name.

2.3 LITERALS

In the statement we saw earlier

```
ADD 1 TO READING-COUNT
```

we have discussed ADD, TO and READING-COUNT; now we are going to discuss the 1. It is an example of what is known in COBOL as a *literal*. Literals are constant values — values which remain unchanged throughout the running of the program. There are three types of literal: numeric literals, like this one, non-numeric literals and figurative constants.

2.3.1 Numeric Literals

Numeric literals are simply numbers very much like the ones we use in everyday life. The precise construction rules for numeric literals are

(1) The characters 0 to 9 may be used

(2) A sign, + or −, may appear immediately before the first character

(3) The decimal point may be used but not as the last character

(4) The maximum size is 18 digits

Figure 2.2 shows some valid and some invalid numeric literals. In this figure, 406 is equivalent to +406, 3 is equivalent to +3 and 10 is equivalent to 10.0. It is purely a question of taste which of each of these alternatives you use. If we look now at the invalid examples, we can see that the first two (3½ and 31,285) contain invalid characters: ½ and comma respectively. + 3 is invalid because, by rule 2, we are not allowed to have a space between the sign and the rest of the literal. Finally 10. infringes rule 3.

invalid	valid	
	+406	406
	−6.2	
3½	3.5	
31,285	31285	
+ 3	+3	3
10.	10.0	10

Figure 2.2   Numeric Literals

2.3.2   Non-numeric Literals

COBOL programs are not just concerned with processing numbers. They also process strings of characters so there is a need for strings of characters with constant values — these are known as *non-numeric literals*. To avoid confusion with COBOL words, they always appear in quotation marks, eg

"SALES STATISTICS"

"10"

"R"

"REORDER NOW !!!!"

Note that since 10 is in quotes it is, in this case, a non-numeric literal not a numeric literal. You might have also noticed in the final example the use of ! which is not in the COBOL character set. In fact you are not restricted to the COBOL character set in non-numeric literals — you can use any character your computer can handle. There is, however, one character that causes a particular problem — the quotation mark. To avoid the danger of a quotation mark within a literal being mistaken, by the compiler, for the end of the literal we must write two quotation marks for every one we want. Thus

"TYPE ""Y"" IF MORE"

has the value: TYPE "Y" IF MORE. With this one restriction any string of characters up to a maximum of 120 is allowed.

2.3.3   Figurative Constants

Obviously there are some constant values which we want to use more often than others. For some such values COBOL has assigned names — known as *figurative constants*. The ones which are most frequently used are SPACE to represent one or more spaces, and ZERO to represent one or more zeros. You can use SPACE anywhere a non-numeric literal is permitted and ZERO anywhere that either type of literal is permitted.

2.4   COBOL FORMATS

Having covered the rules for COBOL words and literals we can now look at the rules for constructing COBOL statements and clauses. A standard notation is used for representing these in most COBOL manuals. Here is an example for the MOVE statement:

$$\underline{\text{MOVE}} \left\{ \begin{array}{l} \text{data-name} \\ \text{literal} \end{array} \right\} \underline{\text{TO}} \text{ data-name}$$

This is known as a *format* for the MOVE statement. It tells us what MOVE statements we are allowed to write. It doesn't tell us anything about the purpose of the MOVE statement or how it works — that comes later.

In the format the underlined words in capitals are *obligatory reserved words*. Thus we must start any MOVE statement with the word MOVE. The braces { } indicate that the programmer has a choice of what to write next — a data-name or a literal. Whichever is chosen, it must be followed by the word TO and a data-name. Thus this format allows us to write, for example

       MOVE BONUS TO PAY

or   MOVE ZERO TO PAY

or   MOVE 0 TO TOTAL-SALES

where BONUS, PAY and TOTAL-SALES are data-names (that is the names given to data items being processed by the program).

This format is a simplified version of the one for the MOVE statement. A more comprehensive format is

$$\underline{\text{MOVE}} \begin{Bmatrix} \text{data-name} \\ \text{literal} \end{Bmatrix} \underline{\text{TO}} \text{ data-name [data-name]} \ldots$$

This differs from the previous format only by the [data-name] . . . on the end. The square brackets indicate that the entry between them is optional. In other words the programmer can choose whether or not to include it in a MOVE statement. The three dots, known as *ellipsis*, indicate that the previous entry may be repeated as many times as desired. So after TO we may have one data-name or two or three or indeed any number of data-names. So according to this format all the following statements are valid

    MOVE BONUS TO PAY

    MOVE ZERO TO PAY

    MOVE 0 TO TOTAL-SALES

    MOVE 0 TO TOTAL-SALES COUNTY-SALES

    MOVE 0 TO TOTAL-SALES COUNTY-SALES REGION-SALES

where BONUS, PAY, TOTAL-SALES, COUNTY-SALES and REGION-SALES are all data-names.

Here is another format (for the LABEL clause):

$$\underline{\text{LABEL}} \begin{Bmatrix} \underline{\text{RECORD}} \text{ IS} \\ \underline{\text{RECORDS}} \text{ ARE} \end{Bmatrix} \begin{Bmatrix} \underline{\text{STANDARD}} \\ \underline{\text{OMITTED}} \end{Bmatrix}$$

This is used in the description of files (as we shall see in the next chapter). It starts with LABEL, an underlined word in capitals, so it is an obligatory reserved word: we must always write it as the first word in this clause. Next we have a choice signified by the braces. We must either choose the top line, RECORD IS, or the bottom one, RECORDS ARE. Similarly we must either choose STANDARD or OMITTED. So we can write

    LABEL RECORD IS STANDARD

    LABEL RECORD IS OMITTED

    LABEL RECORDS ARE STANDARD

or   LABEL RECORDS ARE OMITTED

Since, in the format, all the words are in upper case, they are all reserved words but you might have noticed that the words IS and ARE are not underlined. This means they are *optional words*, in other words you can omit them without changing the meaning of the clause. So you can write

LABEL RECORD STANDARD

and that means precisely the same as

LABEL RECORD IS STANDARD

These optional words are included purely to improve the readability of the program. So provided you are not infringing any of your installation's standards, you can miss them out if you like.

2.5 THE COBOL CODING FORM

COBOL programs are written on real or conceptual coding forms. A sample coding form is shown in figure 2.3. The layout at the top of the page varies considerably but normally makes provision for the specification of such information as the programmer's name and the name of the program. The body of the coding form consists of a number of lines each split up into 80 positions. Although the lines are not required to be 80 positions long this is a widely followed tradition (dating from the days when the standard input medium was punched cards).

The first six positions, known as the *sequence number area*, are reserved for a line number. Since compilers invariably have the capability of numbering the lines when they are listed, many programmers ignore this area. If it is used then it is sensible to allow gaps between the line numbers to allow room for the insertion of extra lines when the program subsequently needs to be amended.

Position 7 on each line is known as the *indicator area* (although many programmers refer to it simply as column 7). It tells the compiler what type of line follows. For normal lines of COBOL it is left blank. An asterisk is used in the indicator area for comment lines — lines which are intended for the human reader and not for the compiler. When the compiler encounters an asterisk in this position it will ignore the whole line apart from printing it in any source listing. A slash in this position also signifies a comment line — the only difference is that the compiler will proceed to the top of the next page before printing it. So it is a way of advancing to a new page in the source listing. Examples of these two comment lines appear in figure 2.4.

In the sample programs that follow, lower-case letters will be used in comments to distinguish them from the rest of the text. This is purely a question of style and on some computers lower-case letters cannot be used with the program.

The next four positions, 8 to 11, are known as *area A*. It is in this area that we start all the headings in our program: division headings, section headings and paragraph headings. These headings can start anywhere in area A. In fact, if you wish you could indent the headings as shown in figure 2.5 to show, for example, that SOURCE-COMPUTER and OBJECT-COMPUTER are part of the section headed CONFIGURATION SECTION which in turn is part of the Environment Division. This is purely a matter of style — the headings must start in area A but it doesn't make any difference to the compiler which position with area A.

The next part of the coding form, from 12 to 72 is referred to as *area B* and it is here that the rest of the COBOL coding appears. For example, the MOVE statements which we saw earlier, since they are not headings, are written in area B. An example is shown on the first line of figure 2.6. We have a lot of freedom about where we write each word in this area:

Program Name . . . .

Author . . . .

Page . . . . of . . . .

NCC

Cobol Coding Form

UMIST

Seq.		Area A		Area B							Ident.
1	6 7 8	11 12	20	30	40	50	60	70 72 73			80

Figure 2.3   A Coding Form

Figure 2.4   Comment Lines

Program Name . . . .

Author . . . .

Page . . . . of . . . .

NCC   Cobol Coding Form   UMIST

Seq. 1 6	7	8	Area A 11 12	Area B 20 30 40 50 60 70 72 73	Ident. 80
	*		THIS IS A COMMENT LINE		
	/		THIS LINE APPEARS AT THE PAGE TOP		
	*		THIS ONE APPEARS ON THE NEXT LINE		

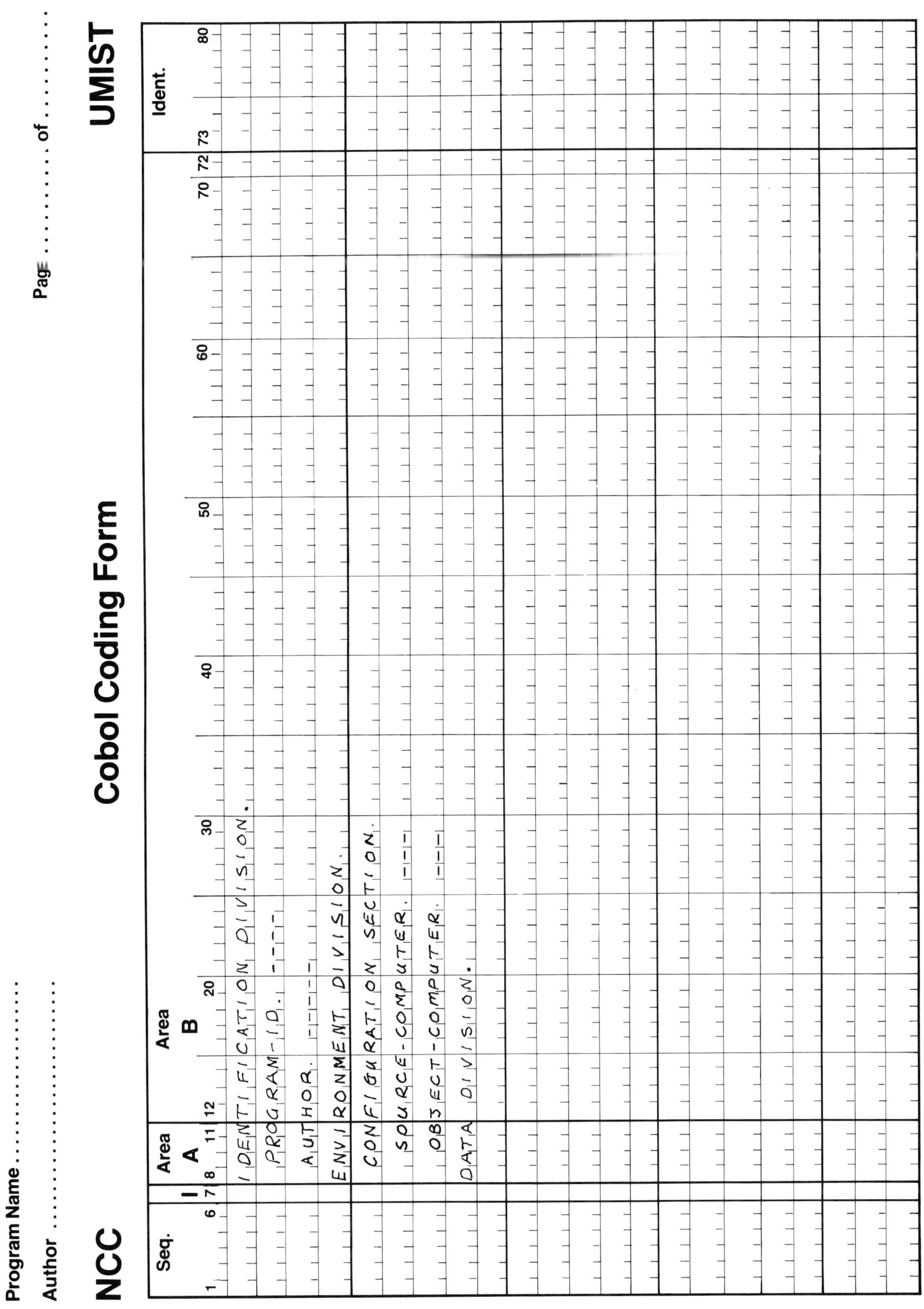

Figure 2.5 Use of Area A

Figure 2.6 Unusual but Valid Spacing

Program Name ....
Author ....

Page .... of ....

NCC   Cobol Coding Form   UMIST

Seq.		Area A	Area B					Ident.
1	6 7 8	11 12	20 30 40 50 60 70 72 73					80
	*		MOVE BONUS TO PAY					
			MAY BE WRITTEN AS FOLLOWS					
			MOVE BONUS					
			TO					
		PAY						

- we can start each line anywhere we like;

- we can leave as many spaces as we like between each word;

- we can go to a new line between any two words;

- we can leave blank lines whenever we like.

Thus the last three lines in figure 2.6 are completely valid and they mean exactly the same as the first line. Obviously there is no point in spreading the MOVE statement out as in this second example. But as we shall see later, we can, in other circumstances, take advantage of this freedom and make our coding easier to read.

Finally, at the end of the coding form we have an *identification area* — columns 73 to 80. This is intended for a code to identify your program but it is not used much these days. When it is used the compiler ignores it.

2.6 SUMMARY

In this chapter we have covered

COBOL characters
COBOL reserved words
COBOL names
Literals
COBOL formats
The use of the COBOL coding form

QUIZ

Some of the questions you will be able to answer from the knowledge you already have. For the others you must refer to the *Reference Summary*. Don't forget to use the index to find your way around.

1. Which of the following are valid *data-names?*

    (a) TOTAL-SALES
    (b) 463
    (c) SON-IN-LAW
    (d) PRICE-IN-£
    (e) CODE=R
    (f) 3C
    (g) ABCDEFGHIJKLMNOPQRSTUVWXYZ
    (h) ETC.
    (i) OVER-TIME-
    (j) A-----9
    (k) FIRST TIME
    (l) BLOCK

2. Which of the following are valid *numeric literals?*

    (a) +4
    (b) 5.
    (c) 0
    (d) 10.11.81.
    (e) TEN
    (f) "9"
    (g) -16E-2
    (h) 3,162.4
    (i) ±3

3. Which of the following are valid *non-numeric literals?*

    (a) "907"
    (b) 907
    (c) "3,162.4"
    (d) "MISSING LINK"
    (e) "LET "X" = 3"
    (f) "£40"
    (g) LET X = "3"
    (h) "OVER-TIME-"

4. Which of the following are valid *figurative constants?*

    (a) SPACES
    (b) QUOTE
    (c) LOW VALUE
    (d) ALL "9"

5. Which of the following are *reserved words* in ANS 74 COBOL?

    (a) ADD
    (b) IS
    (c) I-O-CONTROL
    (d) DEBUG-SUB1
    (e) YES
    (f) DATA-DIVISION
    (g) STATUS

6. Which of the following Procedure Division statements are permitted by the formats shown in the *Reference Summary*? You may assume that ACCOUNTS, INVOICES and METER-READINGS are valid file-names and that OVERTIME and HOURS-WORKED are valid identifiers. The format rules are contained in the *Reference Summary*.

    (a) CLOSE ACCOUNTS METER-READINGS INVOICES
    (b) ADD 35 OVERTIME GIVING HOURS-WORKED
    (c) ADD 35 TO HOURS-WORKED
    (d) ADD 35 TO OVERTIME GIVING HOURS-WORKED
    (e) OPEN OUTPUT ACCOUNTS INVOICES
             INPUT METER-READINGS

OTHER FEATURES

Figurative Constants

When it seems more natural we can write SPACES in place of SPACE. They both mean exactly the same — one or more spaces. The number of spaces they represent depends on the context in which they are used.

Similarly ZEROS and ZEROES can be used as alternatives to ZERO.

HIGH-VALUE (or HIGH-VALUES) can be used when you want the highest possible value and LOW-VALUE (or LOW-VALUES) can be used for the lowest possible value. QUOTE (or QUOTES) can be used as a more convenient way of specifying one or more quotation marks as characters of data.

Finally the figurative constant ALL can be used when a character or string of characters is to be repeated. For example

    ALL "*"

represents a string of asterisks. The length of the string depends on the context in which it is used.

(For more information look up Figurative Constants in the *Reference Summary*.)

3 Defining Files and Records

We now have enough knowledge of the basic rules of COBOL to start writing programs. We are going to start with files, which are fundamental to all data processing applications.

Files are just collections of data. In the electricity office we referred to the file of meter readings, the file of invoices and the customer details file. The details of an individual customer are referred to as a record. So a file consists of a number of records. When we talk about computers some files will be on disks and tapes, others will consist of a computer printout. In fact, any collection of data input from or output to any peripheral is regarded as a file.

In this chapter we will see how files are described in a COBOL program. The example we use is the program which lists the meter readings. In this program we assume the meter readings, which are like the ones used in the electricity company, have been keyed onto disk and that the program is to read them all from disk and list them on a line printer. So we have two files to describe: a meter-reading file on disk and the listing on the printer.

For each file in a COBOL program we must describe the file itself, list the different types of record on the file and list the data items that make up the records. This information is normally contained in the program specification prepared by a systems analyst or a more experienced programmer. So the programmer merely has to translate it into COBOL. Most of the information goes into the File Section of the Data Division but first we must take care of the Select Entries in the Environment Division.

3.1 THE SELECT ENTRY

The Select Entry is used to specify information about the environment in which the file occurs. For this reason it appears in the Environment Division. Figure 3.1 shows Select Entries for the two files in our example.

The Environment Division consists of the Configuration Section, which we have already looked at, and the Input-Output Section which we are concerned with now. The Input-Output Section starts with the two headings INPUT-OUTPUT SECTION and FILE-CONTROL and then we have a Select Entry for each file processed by the program. Each entry has the format

    <u>SELECT</u> file-name
      <u>ASSIGN</u> TO implementor-name.

```
070 ENVIRONMENT DIVISION.
080 CONFIGURATION SECTION.
090 SOURCE-COMPUTER. ANS-2000.
100 OBJECT-COMPUTER. ANS-2000.

110 INPUT-OUTPUT SECTION.
120 FILE-CONTROL.
130     SELECT METER-READINGS ASSIGN TO MTRS35.
140     SELECT METER-LIST ASSIGN TO MTRL25.
```

Figure 3.1 The Environment Division

The file-name is chosen by the programmer and is used throughout the program to identify the file. I have chosen to use the file-names METER-READINGS and METER-LIST for the files in this example. I could have chosen any names subject to the same rules as those that apply to data-names.

Whereas the file-name only has meaning within the program, the implementor-name only has meaning outside it. The file known within the program as METER-READINGS will be known to the Operating System as MTRS35. Thus when this program refers to the file called METER-READINGS this Select Entry will ensure that the file known to the Operating System as MTRS35 is accessed. Similarly, when the file called METER-LIST is referenced, the Operating System will know the file as MTRL25. The precise rules for the construction of the implementor-name vary from one computer to another.

The term implementor will occur fairly frequently in this book. The *implementor* is the person or organisation that produced the compiler. An *implementor-name* is a name which is constructed in accordance with rules provided by the implementor, who will also state the precise meaning of the names.

In the simplest case, such as this, the ASSIGN clause is the only clause needed in the Select Entry but we will encounter other clauses later. Whatever clauses are specified the Entry is always terminated with a full stop.

You will notice from the example in figure 3.1 that the Select Entries are in area B of the coding form. INPUT-OUTPUT SECTION and FILE-CONTROL, like all headings, start in area A.

3.2 FILE DESCRIPTION ENTRIES

The next step in the definition of files is the File Description Entry which appears in the Data Division. The Data Division consists of a number of Sections of which the File Section and the Working Storage Section appear in nearly all programs.

Here we are concerned with the File Section which has the following format:

    FILE SECTION.
    File Description Entry
    Record Description Entries
    File Description Entry
    Record Description Entries
    etc

We shall look first at the File Description Entries which for our sample program are shown in figure 3.2.

```
DATA DIVISION.
FILE SECTION.
FD   METER-READINGS
     LABEL RECORDS STANDARD.
record description
FD   METER-LIST
     LABEL RECORDS OMITTED.
record description.
```

Figure 3.2   File Section of Sample Program

We have one file description entry for each SELECT entry in the program. Each one starts with the reserved word FD (short for file description) in area A. This is followed in area B by the file-name which was used in the corresponding SELECT entry.

There are a number of clauses which can appear after the file-name but only one concerns us at this stage. It is the LABEL RECORDS clause. We specify LABEL RECORDS STANDARD for the disk file which will have a standard label containing the operating system's name for the file and possibly such information as the creation date. However we need not be concerned when we write the COBOL program about the format or contents of the labels. For the printer file which has no labels we write LABEL RECORDS OMITTED. In Standard COBOL the LABEL REC-ORDS clause is compulsory for all files but some implementations do not enforce this rule. The safest rule is to use STANDARD for magnetic files and OMITTED for other files. Note that the FD entries are terminated with full stops. However don't overdo it by putting a full stop after the file-names as well. The LABEL clause may be written on the same line as the FD if you wish.

We have, with the SELECT and FD entries, completed the description of the files. Now we must describe the records which make up these files.

3.3   RECORD DESCRIPTIONS

A file is made up of a collection of records. In the case of the Meter Readings file each Meter Reading is a record. We must now describe the data items in each record and how they are combined to make up the record. Since all the records on the Meter Readings file have the same structure we only need one record description which will apply to all records. The first job is to think of a name for the record (I have chosen METER-READING-REC) and for the data items that make it up: the account number (ACCOUNT-NO), the meter code (METER-CODE) the date (MTR-RDG-DATE) and the reading itself (ACTUAL-READING). The date is made up of the day (MTR-RDG-DAY) the month (MTR-RDG-MONTH) and the year (MTR-RDG-YEAR). The names, shown above in brackets, are known as data-names. These are the names which are used through-out the program when we wish to refer to these data items. Figure 3.3 shows how these data items combine to make up the record.

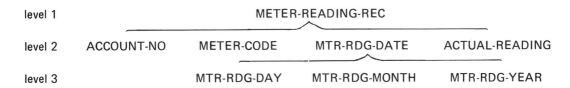

Figure 3.3   Structure of the Meter Reading Record

In this figure, level 1 is the record, level 2 shows the data items that make up the record, and level 3 shows the data items that make up level 2.

We represent this structure in COBOL by listing the data-names with the level number in front of each name: as shown in figure 3.4.

```
1    METER-READING-REC
 2    ACCOUNT-NO
 2    METER-CODE
 2    MTR-RDG-DATE
  3    MTR-RDG-DAY
  3    MTR-RDG-MONTH
  3    MTR-RDG-YEAR
 2    ACTUAL-READING
```

Figure 3.4   A Record Structure in COBOL

We don't have to use level numbers 1 2 3; we could use 1 3 5 as shown in figure 3.5, or 1 10 20. The only rules are that

(i)   we start with 1 for the record and use higher level numbers as we go down the hierarchy

(ii)   all data items on the same level are given the same level number

(iii)   we don't go above level number 49.

```
1    METER-READING-REC
 3    ACCOUNT-NO
 3    METER-CODE
 3    MTR-RDG-DATE
  5    MTR-RDG-DAY
  5    MTR-RDG-MONTH
  5    MTR-RDG-YEAR
 3    ACTUAL-READING
```

Figure 3.5   The Same Record Structure

We interpret figure 3.5 as follows. Level 1 is followed by level 3: therefore the level 1 entry is made up of all the level 3 entries which occur before the next data item with a level number of value lower than 3 (ie 1 or 2) or before we reach the end of the record (as we do in this case). Each of these four level 3s is *subordinate* to the level 1. Similarly the level 3 entry MTR-RDG-DATE is made up of all the level 5 items up to the next entry with a level number with a lower value than 5, in this case ACTUAL-READING. Another way of putting it is that MTR-RDG-DAY, MTR-RDG-MONTH and MTR-RDG-YEAR are subordinate to MTR-RDG-DATE. They are also subordinate to METER-READING-REC.

I shall from now on use level numbers 1, 3, 5, 7, etc. This is common practice amongst programmers because it allows them to insert extra levels into a record without having to alter any of the existing level numbers.

Another question of style is the indentation of the level numbers. Level number 1 must appear in area A of the coding form, and the data-names must appear in area B, but the other level numbers may appear anywhere and can thus be indented as shown in figure 3.5 to emphasise the structure of the record. You will notice also that the data-names have been lined up to make them easier to read.

Before we proceed, there are a few terms we should learn. As you already know, a data item with level 1 is known as a *record*. Any data item which is sub-divided is known as a *group item*. In this case the record itself, METER-READING-REC, and MTR-RDG-DATE are group items. The other items, which are not sub-divided, are known as *elementary items*. In this case ACCOUNT-NO, METER-CODE, MTR-RDG-DAY, MTR-RDG-MONTH, MTR-RDG-YEAR and ACTUAL-READING are elementary items.

3.4 THE PICTURE CLAUSE

So far we have seen how to give names to the data items and link them all together to form the Meter Reading record. But we have said nothing at all about the size of the items or about the type of data they contain — whether, for example, it is numeric or not.

We do both of these tasks with the PICTURE clause which we must use with all the elementary data items. For example, to show that MTR-RDG-DAY consists of two digits we write

    5 MTR-RDG-DAY PICTURE IS 99

Each 9 represents one digit. IS is an optional word and PICTURE may be abbreviated to PIC. So we can instead write

    5 MTR-RDG-DAY PIC 99

The account number consists of eight digits so we write

    3 ACCOUNT-NO PIC 99999999

To save us writing all these 9s (and to make sure we get the correct number of them) we can instead write a single 9 followed, in brackets, by the number of occurrences of it:

    3 ACCOUNT-NO PIC 9(8)

The Meter Code is a five character data item which may contain any characters (letters, digits and others). The Picture Character X is used for such data items and we write

    3 METER-CODE PIC X(5)

Our record definition with all the Picture clauses is shown in figure 3.6.

```
180  1   METER-READING-REC.
190    3   ACCOUNT-NO        PIC 9(8).
200    3   METER-CODE        PIC X(5).
210    3   MTR-RDG-DATE.
220      5 MTR-RDG-DAY       PIC 99.
230      5 MTR-RDG-MONTH     PIC 99.
240      5 MTR-RDG-YEAR      PIC 99.
250    3   ACTUAL-READING    PIC 9(6).
```

Figure 3.6 The Complete Record Description

The items with 9s in the PICTURE clauses are known as *numeric data items* and they may be used for arithmetic if desired. The other items are *alphanumeric data items*, which cannot be used for arithmetic. As well as METER-CODE all group items are regarded as being alphanumeric. Even MTR-RDG-DATE which is made up of numeric data items is regarded as alphanumeric.

The reason we don't have Picture clauses with the group items is that they are unnecessary — the compiler can calculate their lengths. We can see that MTR-RDG-DATE, consisting of three 2-character fields, must be six characters long and the record, METER-READING-REC, is 25 characters long.

The information specified for each data item is known as the *data description entry*. In addition to the level number, data-name and PICTURE there are other clauses we can use in this description as we shall see later. Since we are not going to use any of them here we terminate each of them with a full stop as shown in figure 3.6.

Figure 3.6 shows the complete description for the Meter Reading record. It appears in the program immediately after the Meter Readings File Description entry.

3.5 DEFINING PRINT RECORDS

For printer files each line of print is one record, so we have used the record-name PRINTLINE. Its definition in figure 3.7 shows how it is made up of the Meter Code and a shortened date consisting only of the day and month.


```
1    PRINTLINE.
  3    METER-CODE           PIC X(5).
  3    PL-DATE.
    5    PL-DAY             PIC 99.
    5    PL-MONTH           PIC 99.
```

Figure 3.7   Print Record Definition — First Attempt

The data will be printed exactly as it is stored in the record. Figure 3.8 shows the result of printing several records — each line contains details of one Meter Reading.

```
Y12062204
Y14632204
2X1532304
2X1942304
274AB2304
164AC2404
P13212404
B14232204
146232504
AX4323003
```

Figure 3.8   The Printout — First Attempt

This is unsatisfactory because it is not obvious where the Meter Code ends and the Date begins. We need gaps between the data items.

If we want gaps in the printline we must define them in the print record. For example, if we want a five character gap between METER-CODE and PL-DATE, we must define a data item with PIC X(5) in that position in the print record. Since we never need to store any data in this item we will not need to refer to it — so it doesn't need a name. In these circumstances we can write FILLER in the place where the data-name would appear. This word is reserved for use with such data items.

Figure 3.9 shows the enhanced definition of the print record with a ten character gap at the start of the line, five characters between METER-CODE and PL-DATE, and one character between PL-DAY and PL-MONTH.

```
270 1   PRINTLINE.
280   3 FILLER                PIC X(10).
290   3 METER-CODE            PIC X(5).
300   3 FILLER                PIC X(5).
310   3 PL-DATE.
320     5 PL-DAY              PIC 99.
330     5 FILLER              PIC X.
340     5 PL-MONTH            PIC 99.
350   3 FILLER                PIC X (107).
```

Figure 3.9   Enhanced Print Record Definition

The purpose of the final line in figure 3.9 is to pad the record out to the full length of the printer's line. This padding is required on many computers while others will ensure that the rest of the printline is filled with spaces.

Figure 3.10 shows what the printout will look like now.

```
Y1206          22 04
Y1463          22 04
2X153          23 04
2X194          23 04
274AB          23 04
164AC          24 04
P1321          24 04
B1423          22 04
14623          25 04
AX432          30 03
```

Figure 3.10   The Enhanced Printout

The gaps between the data will not necessarily be filled with spaces as shown here. We, in fact, have to make sure the gaps are filled with spaces. This is a job for the Procedure Division which we shall be looking at in the next chapter.

3.6 SUMMARY

We have now completed the definitions of the two files in our sample program. They are shown together in figure 3.11.

```
        IDENTIFICATION DIVISION.
        PROGRAM-ID. LIST-METER-RDGS-PROGRAM.
       *Author.
       *    J. M. TRIANCE.
       *Function.
       *    This program reads a file of meter readings
       *    and lists the meter code, day and month of
       *    each of them

        ENVIRONMENT DIVISION.
        CONFIGURATION SECTION.
        SOURCE-COMPUTER. ANS-2000.
        OBJECT-COMPUTER. ANS-2000.

        INPUT-OUTPUT SECTION.
        FILE-CONTROL.
            SELECT METER-READINGS ASSIGN TO MTRS4.
            SELECT METER-LIST ASSIGN TO MTRL25.

        DATA DIVISION.
        FILE SECTION.
        FD    METER-READINGS LABEL RECORDS STANDARD.
        1     METER-READING-REC.
          3    ACCOUNT-NO          PIC 9(8).
          3    METER-CODE          PIC X(5).
          3    MTR-RDG-DATE.
            5 MTR-RDG-DAY          PIC 99.
            5 MTR-RDG-MONTH        PIC 99.
            5 MTR-RDG-YEAR         PIC 99.
          3    ACTUAL-READING      PIC 9(6).
        FD    METER-LIST LABEL RECORDS OMITTED.
        1     PRINTLINE.
          3    FILLER              PIC X(10).
          3    METER-CODE          PIC X(5).
          3    FILLER              PIC X(5).
          3    PL-DATE.
            5 PL-DAY               PIC 99.
            5 FILLER               PIC X.
            5 PL-MONTH             PIC 99.
          3    FILLER              PIC X(107).
```

Figure 3.11 The First Three Divisions of the Sample Program

QUIZ

1. List the errors in the following coding extract

```
1     INPUT-OUTPUT SECTION.
2         SELECT STOCK-FILE ASSIGN STOCKMAST
3         SELECT REORDER-FILE ASSIGN REORDER.
4     FILE SECTION.
5     FD  STOCK-FILE.
6         LABLE RECORDS STANDARD.
7         1   STOCK-REC.
8         3   STOCK-CODE      PIC 999
9         3   DESCRIPTION     PIC X(40).
10        5   SHORT-DESCR     PIC X(10).
11        5   LONG-DESCR      PIC X(30).
12        3   STOCK LEVEL.
13    FD  REORDER
14        LABEL RECORDS STANDARD.
          .
          .
          .
```

2. What clause in the File Description Entry is compulsory?

3. List five other clauses which can appear in the File Description Entry (see the *Reference Summary*).

4. What level numbers can be used to specify the structure of a record?

5. In the following record

```
1     EMPLOYEE-DETAILS.
  3   EMP-NUMBER        PIC 9(4).
  3   EMP-NAME          PIC X(30).
  3   EMP-ADDRESS.
    5 STREET            PIC X(30).
    5 TOWN              PIC X(20).
    5 POSTAL-CODE       PIC X(7).
  3   SALARY            PIC 9(5).
```

how many characters of storage do EMP-NUMBER, EMP-ADDRESS and EMPLOYEE-DETAILS occupy?

6. In the record in question 5 state the record name and the names of the group items.

7. What is the name for data items which are not group items?

8. Abbreviate the following as much as possible

   PICTURE IS 9999999

9. What special word can be used in place of a data-name in a description entry when the data item is never referred to from elsewhere in the program?

OTHER FEATURES

1.   Other File Description Clauses

You should be aware of the other file description clauses. LABEL RECORDS has already been discussed and LINAGE will be covered later. Two of the other clauses, RECORD CONTAINS and DATA RECORDS, are purely for documentation in Standard COBOL — in other words the compiler ignores them. The BLOCK CONTAINS clause is used to specify the size of the blocks of data in which the records are stored in the file. On some computers this clause can make a great difference to the efficiency of the program, on others it can be overriden by the operating system. The VALUE OF clause also varies in importance from being obligatory for some files in some implementations to being completely ignored in others.

(For more information look up File Description Entry in the *Reference Summary*.)

2.   The COPY Statement

As you can no doubt imagine it is very tedious writing out long record definitions. If the same record is used in several programs it is even more tedious and as a result there is an increased like-lihood that mistakes will be made. The *COBOL library* facility is designed to overcome these problems. It can be used for storing program extracts in a library on backing store and copying them in whenever they are required. For example, the record definition in figure 3.6 could be stored in the library. When we do this we must give it a name, known as a *text-name*: let's call it COMPLETE-METER-RDG. Then in the program we could write

```
            .
            .
            .
FD       METER-RDGS
             LABEL RECORDS STANDARD.
         COPY COMPLETE-METER-RDG.
FD       METER-LIST
            .
            .
            .
```

The COPY statement would be replaced by the contents of COMPLETE-METER-RDG which would then be processed by the compiler as if they had been written by the programmer.

(For more information look up COPY in the *Reference Summary*.)

4 The Procedure Division

In the last chapter we finished the Environment Division and wrote the Data Division in our sample program. In so doing we described the two files we are processing and the records they contain. However, we have not yet told the computer what we want it to do with these files. We must instruct it to read each record in turn from the Meter Readings file and print the required details. This is done in the Procedure Division.

4.1 PROCEDURE DIVISION STRUCTURE

The Procedure Division is made up of paragraphs and each paragraph is made up of paragraph-name followed by a full stop and then by zero or more statements followed by a full stop (as shown in figure 4.1).

```
PROCEDURE DIVISION.
paragraph-name.           ⎫
     [statement ... .]    ⎬  a paragraph
                          ⎭
paragraph-name.
     [statement ... .]
          .
          .
          .
          .
```

Figure 4.1 Basic Format of Procedure Division

The paragraph-names are names chosen by the programmer according to the same rules as the data-names except that purely numeric names (such as 10 or 15) may be used if desired. There is a different type of statement for each operation we wish to perform (moving data, adding, reading, writing, etc). The one thing they have in common is that they all start with a COBOL verb (MOVE, ADD, READ, WRITE, etc). We shall discuss each of these different verbs in due course.

Returning to our sample program we must now work out what we need to do in its Procedure Division. As with any program there is some Initial Processing and Terminal Processing and between these we must process each record. Processing a record involves reading the record from the disk file, moving the data to the printline record and then printing the printline record. We thus have the following structure.

Initial Processing (including reading the first record)
Process records
     ie for each record   set up the printline
                              print the printline
                              read the next record
Terminal Processing

For this simple program one paragraph will suffice, let's call it LIST-METER-READINGS. Figure 4.2 shows an outline of the COBOL Procedure Division containing the paragraph-name and the file processing statements.

```
PROCEDURE DIVISION.
LIST-METER-READINGS.

*Initial processing
      OPEN INPUT METER-READINGS
      READ METER-READINGS
      OPEN OUTPUT METER-LIST

*Process records
*     For each record
*           Set up printline
      WRITE PRINTLINE
      READ METER-READINGS

*Terminal processing
      CLOSE METER-READINGS METER-LIST
```

Figure 4.2   Outline of Procedure Division

Note in this program how spacing and comment lines (*Initial processing, *Process records and *Terminal Processing) are used to show the structure of the program. Comment lines (*For each record, *Set up printline) are also used to temporarily represent logic which has not yet been expressed in COBOL.

Before we complete this Procedure Division, however, we will look at each of the four file processing verbs we have used: OPEN, CLOSE, READ and WRITE.

4.2   THE OPEN STATEMENT

Before we can do anything else with a file we must 'open' it just as in the manual equivalent we must open a filing cabinet before we can process the records in it. Thus in most COBOL programs you will open all the files at the beginning and, in fact, close them all at the end.

A simplified format of the OPEN statement is

$$\text{OPEN} \quad \begin{Bmatrix} \underline{\text{INPUT}} \\ \underline{\text{OUTPUT}} \end{Bmatrix} \quad \text{file-name}$$

The word INPUT is used for files which are to be transferred into the central store of the computer and OUTPUT for ones which are transferred from the central store. The file-name is the same one that we have already used immediately after the reserved words SELECT and FD. Thus for the two files in our sample program we write

                    OPEN INPUT METER-READINGS

and

                    OPEN OUTPUT METER-LIST

The action taken by the computer varies from computer to computer and peripheral to peripheral. For an input disk file, the OPEN statement would, for example, find the file by looking in the file directory. However the programmer need not be concerned with the action of the statement — all you have to do is OPEN each file before it is used.

4.3 THE CLOSE STATEMENT

Just as we must open all files before we use them so also must we close them when we have finished processing them. We do this with the CLOSE statement the format of which is

                    CLOSE file-name-1 [file-name-2] ...

so to close our two files we simply write

                    CLOSE METER-READINGS METER-LIST

Some programmers like to line up the file-names under each other:

                    CLOSE METER-READINGS
                          METER-LIST

They are of course free to do this since as with any two COBOL words, the space between METER-READINGS and METER-LIST can be made as large as you like, even to the extent of putting them on different lines.

4.4 THE READ STATEMENT

The READ statement is used to transfer a record from a file into the record area allocated for it in main storage. This is the record area described after the File Description entry. The basic format for READ is

    READ file-name RECORD
           AT END imperative-statement
    END-READ

We will look at the AT END phrase shortly. For the time being we will write

        READ METER-READINGS

to obtain the next record in sequence from this file. After executing this statement the various data items in the record can be accessed by referring to the data-names (ACCOUNT-NO, etc) in the associated record — METER-READINGS-REC (see figure 4.3).

4.5 THE WRITE STATEMENT

After all the information has been moved into the printer record PRINTLINE (and we'll see how to do that in a moment) we are ready to print it. Transferring a record from the central store to a printer is done, in the same way as transferring records to any peripheral, by using a WRITE statement. Its basic format is

    WRITE record-name

where record-name appears in a level 1 entry after the FD entry for the file in question.

Note that unlike OPEN, CLOSE and READ you must specify the record-name not the file-name. This is because, as you will see later, there is often more than one type of record on a file and it is then necessary to indicate which type is to be written.

For our sample program we write

WRITE PRINTLINE

to ensure that the current contents of the record PRINTLINE are transferred to the next line on the printer.

4.6   RELATIONSHIP TO DATA DIVISION

You will note that when coding the Procedure Division we make frequent reference to the Data Division. Thus for your convenience the Data Division of our sample program, which we wrote in the last chapter, is reproduced in figure 4.3.

```
DATA DIVISION.
FILE SECTION.
FD      METER-READINGS LABEL RECORDS STANDARD.
1       METER-READING-REC.
    3   ACCOUNT-NO      PIC 9(8).
    3   METER-CODE      PIC X(5).
    3   MTR-RDG-DATE.
      5 MTR-RDG-DAY     PIC 99.
      5 MTR-RDG-MONTH   PIC 99.
      5 MTR-RDG-YEAR    PIC 99.
    3   ACTUAL-READING  PIC 9(6).
FD      METER-LIST LABEL RECORDS OMITTED.
1       PRINTLINE.
    3   FILLER          PIC X(10).
    3   METER-CODE      PIC X(5).
    3   FILLER          PIC X(5).
    3   PL-DATE.
      5 PL-DAY          PIC 99.
      5 FILLER          PIC X.
      5 PL-MONTH        PIC 99.
    3   FILLER          PIC X(107).
```

Figure 4.3   Data Division of Sample Program

4.7   THE MOVE STATEMENT

This copies data from one part of main storage to another. The full format for MOVE is rather involved so we will start with a simplified version and work our way up. The simplest form is:

MOVE data-name-1 TO data-name-2

The action of this statement is to copy the contents of data-name-1 into data-name-2. Thus the original contents of data-name-2 are completely overwritten, while the contents of data-name-1 remain unaltered (thus in normal English we are actually 'copying' the data rather than 'moving' it).

For example in our sample program we can write

```
MOVE MTR-RDG-DAY TO PL-DAY
```

If MTR-RDG-DAY contains 13 and PL-DAY contains 10, then after the execution of this statement, MTR-RDG-DAY will still contain 13 but PL-DAY will now contain 13 as well. Likewise for transferring the month we write

```
MOVE MTR-RDG-MONTH TO PL-MONTH
```

4.8 QUALIFIERS

To transfer the meter code we might write

```
MOVE METER-CODE TO METER-CODE
```

This of course looks very confusing to us and it would confuse the compiler as well. Since we have used the same data-name in two different places we must tell the compiler that the first METER-CODE is in METER-READING-REC and the second one is in PRINTLINE.

We do this by simply writing

```
MOVE METER-CODE IN METER-READING-REC
    TO METER-CODE IN PRINTLINE
```

In this statement METER-CODE IN METER-READING-REC is an example of a *qualified data-name* with METER-READING-REC being known as a *qualifier*. You can use OF as an alternative to IN in qualified data-names.

Strictly speaking this last move statement no longer satisfies the format for MOVE given in the previous section. The actual format for MOVE uses the word identifier rather than data-name. So our simplest format becomes

```
MOVE identifier-1 TO identifier-2
```

Whenever identifier appears in a format you can write a data-name or a qualified data-name.

You can of course always avoid the use of qualifiers by making all data-names unique. In the above example we could have used MTR-RDG-METER-CODE and PL-METER-CODE in place of the two instances of METER-CODE. The approach taken is a question of style.

4.9 MOVING LITERALS

Besides moving data items it is also possible to move literals by writing statements of the following form

```
MOVE literal TO identifier
```

Any literal may be used: numeric, non-numeric or a figurative constant.

We need a MOVE of this format in our sample program to clear the printline. At the beginning of the program the printline will contain whatever data happens to have been left in that particular location by the previous program. Since nothing is moved into the FILLER data items this would get printed (see Figure 4.4 where colons happen to be stored in the FILLER items).

```
: : : : : : : : : :Y1206: : : : :22:04: : : : : : : : : : : : : : : : : : : : : : : : : : : : : : : : :
: : : : : : : : : :Y1463: : : : :22:04: : : : : : : : : : : : : : : : : : : : : : : : : : : : : : : : :
: : : : : : : : : :2X153: : : : :23:04: : : : : : : : : : : : : : : : : : : : : : : : : : : : : : : : :
: : : : : : : : : :2X194: : : : :23:04: : : : : : : : : : : : : : : : : : : : : : : : : : : : : : : : :
: : : : : : : : : :274AB: : : : :23:04: : : : : : : : : : : : : : : : : : : : : : : : : : : : : : : : :
: : : : : : : : : :164AC: : : : :24:04: : : : : : : : : : : : : : : : : : : : : : : : : : : : : : : : :
: : : : : : : : : :P1321: : : : :24:04: : : : : : : : : : : : : : : : : : : : : : : : : : : : : : : : :
: : : : : : : : : :B1423: : : : :22:04: : : : : : : : : : : : : : : : : : : : : : : : : : : : : : : : :
: : : : : : : : : :14623: : : : :25:04: : : : : : : : : : : : : : : : : : : : : : : : : : : : : : : : :
: : : : : : : : : :AX432: : : : :30:03: : : : : : : : : : : : : : : : : : : : : : : : : : : : : : : : :
```

Figure 4.4   Printout with Uncleared Printline

The easiest way to ensure that the gaps are clear is to space fill the whole record. We can do that by writing

```
MOVE SPACES TO PRINTLINE
```

before we move anything else into the record. This will then ensure the report is as shown in figure 3.10.

After adding the above statements, the Process records routine becomes:

```
*Process records
*       For each record
            MOVE SPACES TO PRINTLINE
            MOVE METER-CODE OF METER-READING-REC
              TO METER-CODE OF PRINTLINE
            MOVE MTR-RDG-DAY TO PL-DAY
            MOVE MTR-RDG-MONTH TO PL-MONTH
            WRITE PRINTLINE
            READ METER-READINGS
```

Thus, for each record, the printline is cleared, the three data items are moved from the meter reading record to the printline, the printline is written and the next record is read.

This now leaves us with the task of expressing in COBOL the logic 'for each record'. In other words we must ensure that the above coding is executed once for each record.

4.10 THE IN-LINE PERFORM STATEMENT

The PERFORM statement is used when some coding is to be repeated. Here we will use the in-line format:

PERFORM UNTIL condition

statement ...

END-PERFORM

The statements embedded between PERFORM and END-PERFORM are repeated until the condition is true. The condition is tested *before* each execution of the set of statements, and when it is true execution of the PERFORM statement is complete, and the computer executes the next statement (after END-PERFORM).

The rules for conditions in COBOL are given later. In the case of our sample program the condition will test for the end of the meter readings file, so the PERFORM statement could take the following form:

```
PERFORM UNTIL END-OF-FILE-FLAG = "Y"
statements to process 1 record
END-PERFORM
```

In this example it is assumed that END-OF-FILE-FLAG is a data-item which will have "Y" stored in it when the end of the meter readings file has been reached.

4.11 HANDLING THE END OF FILE

The end of file is detected by the AT END branch of the read statement. In this case the following READ statement is needed.

```
READ METER-READINGS
    AT END MOVE "Y" TO END-OF-FILE-FLAG
END-READ
```

This statement is of the form:

READ file-name RECORD

      AT END statement ...

END-READ

The END-READ is needed to mark the end of the set of embedded statements. Terminators of this form are used with all statements in which any of the code is conditional: in this case the statements following AT END are only executed when there are no more records in the file.

The end of file processing is thus handled by the following code:

```
*Initial processing
        :
    MOVE "N" TO END-OF-FILE-FLAG
    READ METER-READINGS
      AT END MOVE "Y" TO END-OF-FILE-FLAG
    END-READ

*Process records
    PERFORM UNTIL END-OF-FILE-FLAG = "Y"
*       :
*       statements to process one record
*       :
      READ METER-READINGS
        AT END MOVE "Y" TO END-OF-FILE-FLAG
      END-READ
    END-PERFORM
```

Note that the data item END-OF-FILE-FLAG is initially given a value "N" to indicate that the end of file has not yet been encountered. The first record is then read or, if the file is empty, the end of file flag is set (to "Y"). If the file is not empty the first record is processed and an attempt is made to read the second record. Each of the records on the file is processed in turn and when the file is finished the computer proceeds to the statement after END-PERFORM.

END-OF-FILE-FLAG, like all other data items, must be defined in the Data Division. Since it is not input to or output from the program it does not appear in the File Section. Instead it appears in the Working-Storage Section (which is discussed more in the next chapter):

```
WORKING-STORAGE SECTION.
1 END-OF-FILE-FLAG PIC X.
```

4.12 THE STOP RUN STATEMENT

The STOP RUN statement is used to tell the computer that the program has finished. It is thus always the very last statement executed. In our sample program it will appear after the CLOSE statement:

```
CLOSE METER-READINGS METER-LIST
STOP RUN
```

STOP RUN is, in this case, physically the last line of coding in the program but as we shall see later it can appear anywhere in the Procedure Division. No special COBOL word or statement is used to mark the physical end of the COBOL program.

4.13 THE COMPLETE PROGRAM

We have now completed our first COBOL program. It is shown in full in figure 4.5.

```
1       IDENTIFICATION DIVISION.
2       PROGRAM-ID. LIST-METER-RDGS-PROGRAM.
3       *Author.
4       *    J. M. TRIANCE.
5       *Function.
6       *    This program reads a file of meter readings
7       *    and lists the meter code, day and month of
8       *    each of them
9
10      ENVIRONMENT DIVISION.
11      CONFIGURATION SECTION.
12      SOURCE-COMPUTER. ANS-2000.
13      OBJECT-COMPUTER. ANS-2000.
14
15      INPUT-OUTPUT SECTION.
16      FILE-CONTROL.
17          SELECT METER-READINGS ASSIGN TO MTRS4.
18          SELECT METER-LIST ASSIGN TO MTRL25.
19
20      DATA DIVISION.
21      FILE SECTION.
22      FD      METER-READINGS LABEL RECORDS STANDARD.
23      1       METER-READING-REC.
24          3   ACCOUNT-NO          PIC 9(8).
25          3   METER-CODE          PIC X(5).
26          3   MTR-RDG-DATE.
27            5 MTR-RDG-DAY          PIC 99.
28            5 MTR-RDG-MONTH        PIC 99.
29            5 MTR-RDG-YEAR         PIC 99.
30          3   ACTUAL-READING      PIC 9(6).
31      FD      METER-LIST LABEL RECORDS OMITTED.
32      1       PRINTLINE.
33          3   FILLER              PIC X(10).
34          3   METER-CODE          PIC X(5).
35          3   FILLER              PIC X(5).
36          3   PL-DATE.
37            5 PL-DAY              PIC 99.
38            5 FILLER              PIC X.
```

(Figure 4.5 continues)

```
39        5 PL-MONTH              PIC 99.
40      3   FILLER                PIC X(107).
41
42   WORKING-STORAGE SECTION.
43   1      END-OF-FILE-FLAG     PIC X.
44
45   PROCEDURE DIVISION.
46   LIST-METER-READINGS.
47
48  *Initial processing
49        OPEN INPUT METER-READINGS
50        MOVE "N" TO END-OF-FILE-FLAG
51        READ METER-READINGS
52          AT END MOVE "Y" TO END-OF-FILE-FLAG
53        END-READ
54        OPEN OUTPUT METER-LIST
55
56  *Process records
57        PERFORM UNTIL END-OF-FILE-FLAG = "Y"
58             MOVE SPACES TO PRINTLINE
59             MOVE METER-CODE OF METER-READING-REC
60               TO METER-CODE OF PRINTLINE
61             MOVE MTR-RDG-DAY TO PL-DAY
62             MOVE MTR-RDG-MONTH TO PL-MONTH
63             WRITE PRINTLINE
64             READ METER-READINGS
65               AT END MOVE "Y" TO END-OF-FILE-FLAG
66             END-READ
67        END-PERFORM
68
69  *Terminal processing
70        CLOSE METER-READINGS METER-LIST
71        STOP RUN.
```

Figure 4.5   A Complete COBOL Program

If you look at the Procedure Division you will notice that we have used full stops:

— after the PROCEDURE DIVISION heading

— after the paragraph-name

— at the end of the paragraph

All these full stops are necessary.

You will also note that the Division header and the paragraph-names all start in area-A while the rest of the coding is in area-B of the coding form. This too is obligatory.

4.14 A SIMULATION OF THE PROGRAM

This section shows the effect of executing the program for a meter reading file containing the following two records:

	Account No	Meter Code	Date	Reading
Record 1	71325879	Y1206	220480	008915
Record 2	71654321	Y1463	220480	014365

The purpose of this exercise is to clear up any lingering doubts or misconceptions you might have about how the statements actually work. It also demonstrates a method which can be used for checking any piece of code which you are uncertain of.

The diagram used (see figure 4.6) shows the central store of the computer, the disk which contains METER-READINGS and the printer which is to be used for METER-LIST. Within the store the records METER-READING-REC and PRINTLINE are shown. Each is divided up into individual characters although there is insufficient space to show the unused character positions on the end of PRINTLINE. Also shown is data item END-OF-FILE-FLAG.

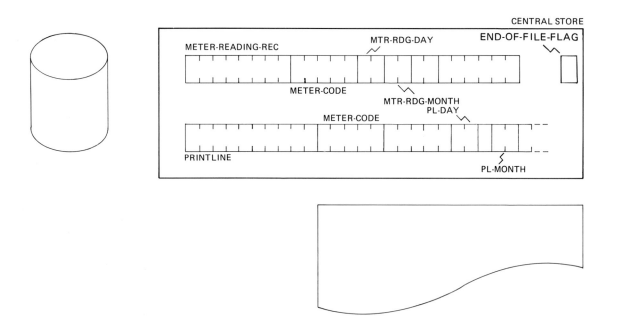

Figure 4.6   Files and Records used in the Program

Figure 4.7 shows the state after the two files have been opened. METER READINGS file will have been located on the disk and the printer will be standing by to receive METER-LIST. The record areas will still contain whatever data was left there from the previous run.

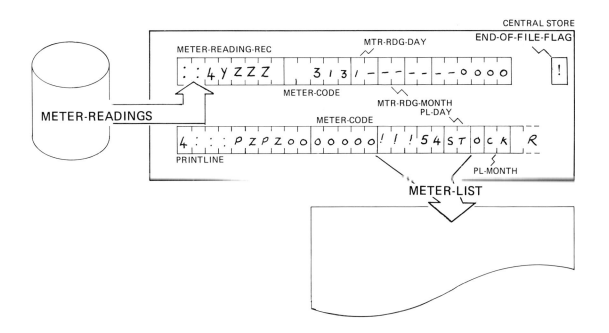

Figure 4.7   After Opening the Files

The MOVE statement on line 50 will store N in END-OF-FILE-FLAG.

After executing the READ statement the first record from METER-READINGS will be in METER-READING-REC (figure 4.8). Since it is not the end of the file, the MOVE statement on line 52 will not be executed.

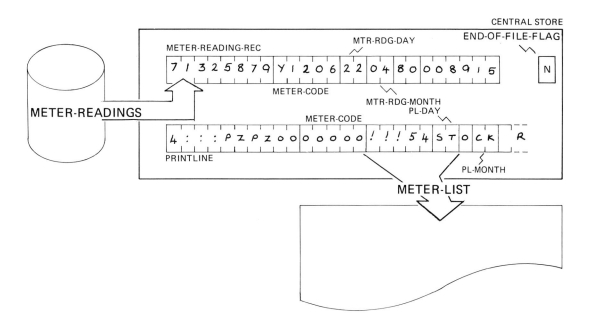

Figure 4.8   After the First READ

Since the condition following UNTIL is not true (END-OF-FILE-FLAG does not contain Y) the statements within the PERFORM statement are executed (lines 58 to 66).

When MOVE SPACES TO PRINTLINE is executed PRINTLINE becomes clear (figure 4.9).

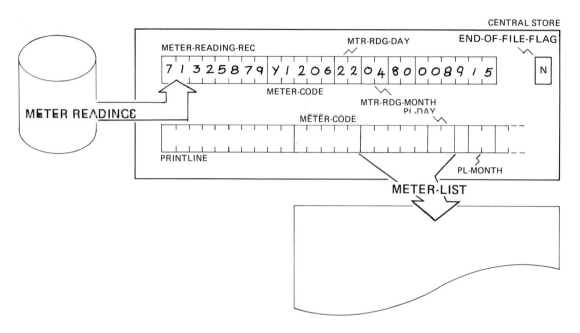

Figure 4.9   After Moving Spaces to PRINTLINE

Next we execute MOVE METER-CODE OF METER-READING-REC TO METER-CODE OF PRINTLINE (figure 4.10).

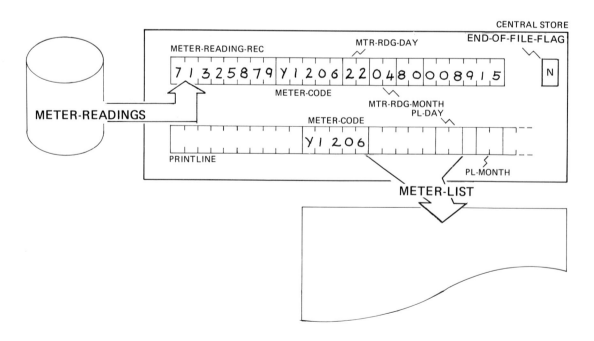

Figure 4.10   After Moving the Meter Code

After executing MOVE MTR-RDG-DAY TO PL-DAY and MOVE MTR-RDG-MONTH TO PL-MONTH the print line is complete (figure 4.11).

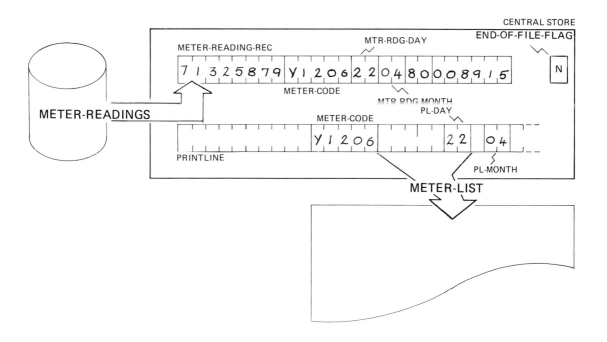

Figure 4.11   A Complete Printline Record

The WRITE statement transfers the contents of PRINTLINE to the printer (figure 4.12).

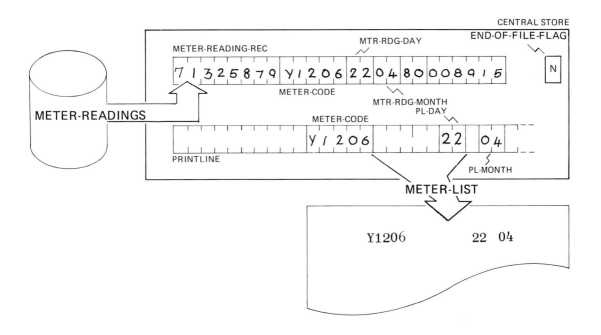

Figure 4.12   After the WRITE statement

The READ statement on lines 64 to 66 obtains the second record and since END-PERFORM comes next the PERFORM condition is re-tested to see if its embedded statements (lines 58 to 66) should be executed again. Since the condition is false, they are; with the result that the second record is processed and an attempt is made to read the third record. Figure 4.13 shows the effect of executing this sequence of statements (lines 58 to 66) a second time.

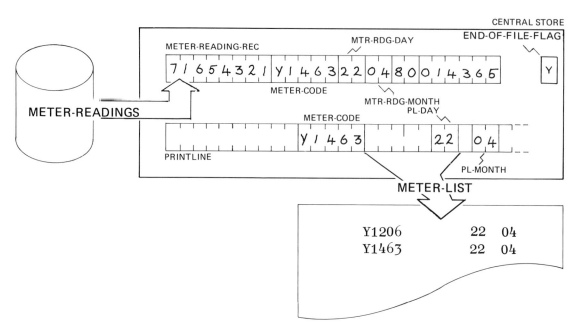

Figure 4.13   After Second Execution of PROCESS-RECORDS Paragraph

Note that, since there is no third record on the file, this last attempt to read fails and the AT END coding is executed: in other words, "Y" is moved to END-OF-FILE-FLAG.

After executing the READ statements the PERFORM condition is re-tested and on this occasion is true. So the computer proceeds to the next statement (after END-PERFORM) where the files are closed and the program terminates with STOP RUN.

4.15 SUMMARY

In this chapter we have seen the structure of a Procedure Division and have had an introduction to the following statement formats.

OPEN $\left\{ \begin{array}{c} \underline{\text{INPUT}} \\ \underline{\text{OUTPUT}} \end{array} \right\}$ file-name

CLOSE file-name-1 [file-name-2] ...

READ file-name RECORD

    AT END statement ...

END-READ

WRITE record-name

MOVE $\left\{ \begin{array}{c} \text{identifier-1} \\ \text{literal} \end{array} \right\}$ TO identifier-2

PERFORM UNTIL condition

    statement ...

END-PEFORM

STOP RUN

Finally, we simulated the action of the computer to see exactly what happens when the program is executed.

QUIZ

1. List the errors in the following Procedure Division Coding:

```
 1    PROCEDURE DIVISION.
 2        OPEN STOCK-FILE
 3        OPEN STOCK-FILE-COPY
 4        READ STOCK-FILE
 5        PERFORM UNTIL END-FILE-FLAG = "Y"
 6        MOVE STOCK REC TO STOCK-COPY-REC
 7        WRITE STOCK-FILE-COPY
 8        END-PERFORM
 9        CLOSE STOCK-FILE
10    STOP RUN.
```

2. Given the following files:

DISK-IN	— disk input file
TAPE-IN	— magnetic tape input file
DISK-OUT	— disk output file
PRINT-FILE	— printer file

    indicate which of the following statements are valid. (Don't forget to use the *Reference Summary*.)

    (a)   OPEN INPUT DISK-IN
    (b)   OPEN OUTPUT DISK-OUT PRINT-FILE
    (c)   OPEN INPUT TAPE-IN OUTPUT DISK-OUT
    (d)   CLOSE INPUT TAPE-IN OUTPUT DISK-OUT
    (e)   OPEN OUTPUT DISK-OUT INPUT TAPE-IN
    (f)   OPEN INPUT PRINT-FILE

3. Which of the verbs we have covered in this chapter would you use for the following circumstances?

    (a)   to get a file ready for reading or writing
    (b)   to transfer a record from magnetic tape to central store
    (c)   to transfer a record from central store to disk
    (d)   to transfer a record directly from magnetic tape to disk
    (e)   to transfer data from one part of central store to another
    (f)   to store a literal value in a data item
    (g)   to repeatedly execute a sequence of statements
    (h)   to detect the end of an input file
    (i)   to indicate that processing of a file has finished
    (j)   to terminate the program

4. Given the data definitions:

```
1   STOCK-CODE.
 3  ALPHA-CODE      PIC XX.
 3  NUM-CODE        PIC 99.
1   CODE-STORE      PIC XX.
```

    which of the following MOVE statements are valid? (When reading the *Reference Summary* you can ignore non-integer and edited data items at this stage.)

(a)   MOVE ALPHA-CODE TO CODE-STORE
(b)   MOVE SPACES TO ALPHA-CODE CODE-STORE
(c)   MOVE ZEROS TO ALPHA-CODE CODE-STORE NUM-CODE
(d)   MOVE NUM-CODE TO CODE-STORE
(e)   MOVE CODE-STORE TO NUM-CODE
(f)   MOVE SPACES TO NUM-CODE
(g)   MOVE SPACES TO STOCK-CODE
(h)   MOVE ALPHA-CODE OF STOCK-CODE TO CODE-STORE
(i)   MOVE "13" TO CODE-STORE

5.   Given the File Section:

```
FD    METER-READINGS LABEL RECORDS STANDARD.
1     METER-READING-REC.
  3    ACCOUNT-NO            PIC 9(8).
  3    METER-CODE            PIC X(5).
  3    RDG-DATE.
    5 DAY                    PIC 99.
    5 MONTH                  PIC 99.
    5 YEAR                   PIC 99.
  3    ACTUAL READING        PIC 9(6).
FD    SUMMARY-FILE LABEL RECORDS STANDARD.
1     SUMMARY-REC.
  3    METER-CODE            PIC X(5).
  3    RDG-DATE.
    5 DAY                    PIC 99.
    5 MONTH                  PIC 99.
```

which of the following are valid identifiers? (You may assume that none of these names is used anywhere else in the program.)

(a)   ACCOUNT-NO
(b)   METER-CODE
(c)   METER-CODE OF SUMMARY-REC
(d)   DAY OF RDG-DATE
(e)   YEAR OF RDG-DATE
(f)   MONTH OF RDG-DATE IN SUMMARY-REC
(g)   MONTH OF METER-READING-REC
(h)   METER-CODE OF SUMMARY-FILE

OTHER FEATURES

1.   OPEN EXTEND

Sometimes you want to add records to the end of an existing file rather than starting a new file. This can be done by the EXTEND option of OPEN.

2.   MOVE CORRESPONDING

Normally, in a MOVE from one group item to another, both group items are regarded as simple alphanumeric strings and moved as such without regard to the data items that make up the groups. In our sample program, when we wanted to move elementary items within a group we wrote a separate MOVE for each elementary item. However, if we give the same name to the source data items and the destination data item in each MOVE we can achieve the same effect with a single MOVE. For example in the records in exercise 5, we can move the METER-CODE, DAY and MONTH from METER-READING-REC to SUMMARY-REC by writing

MOVE CORRESPONDING METER–READING–REC TO SUMMARY–REC.

This feature can save a lot of coding when used in favourable circumstances. However some programmers dislike it because they have to use qualifiers when they wish to refer to the moved data items elsewhere in the program.

(For more information look up CORRESPONDING option in the *Reference Summary*.)

5 Filling In Some Gaps

One of the objectives of this book has been to write our first COBOL program as quickly as possible so that you could get an overview of the language at an early stage. To achieve this objective a very simple problem was selected for this program. As a result it was, in some respects, untypical of the COBOL programs normally written.

In this chapter we are going to write a more typical program. It is based on the original problem with the following changes:

1. The Meter Readings File is going to contain two different types of record but we are only going to print one type.

2. A heading is going to be printed at the beginning of the report.

3. A line containing the total number of records read and the total number printed is going to be printed at the end of the report (see figure 5.1).

These changes require the following new COBOL features

Multiple Record Types

Constant Values

Addition

Comparisons

```
READING DATES
        Y1206        22  04
        Y1463        22  04
        2X153        23  04
        2X194        23  04
        274AB        23  04
        164AC        24  04
        P1321        24  04
        B1423        22  04
        14623        25  04
        AX432        30  03
NO. OF READINGS = 0010        NO. OF RECORDS = 0013
```

Figure 5.1 The Enhanced Printout

47

5.1 MULTIPLE RECORD LAYOUTS

When there are two record layouts on a file we simply define them one after the other in the file section as in figure 5.2. You will notice that the Meter Reading Record is as before except for the addition of the data item RECORD-CODE. This contains a code which distinguishes the Meter Reading Records from the other type of record — the Fault Record. RECORD-CODE contains "R" in the case of Reading records and "F" in the case of Fault Records.

```
DATA DIVISION.
FILE SECTION.
FD   METER-READINGS LABEL RECORDS STANDARD.
1    METER-READING-REC.
  3   RECORD-CODE     PIC X.
  3   ACCOUNT-NO      PIC 9(8).
  3   METER-CODE      PIC X(5).
  3   MTR-RDG-DATE.
    5 MTR-RDG-DAY     PIC 99.
    5 MTR-RDG-MONTH   PIC 99.
    5 MTR-RDG-YEAR    PIC 99.
  3   ACTUAL-READING  PIC 9(6).
1    METER-FAULT-REC.
  3   FILLER          PIC X.
  3   FAULT-CODE      PIC X(5).
  3   FAULT-DETAILS   PIC X(20).
FD   METER-LIST LABEL RECORDS OMITTED.
        .
        .
        .
```

Figure 5.2   Definition of Two Record Layouts on one File

If you add up the size of the two types of record you will see that they are both 26 characters. We can cope with different lengthed records in the same file but we will save that complication until later in the book.

When there was only one record type all the records were read one at a time into the same area of central storage. The same is true when we have two or more record types — enough storage is reserved for only one record*. This record area is viewed in one of two ways depending on which type of record currently resides in it. Figure 5.3 shows the single record area. Above it is shown the definition for when it contains a Meter Reading Record and below it is shown the definition for when it contains a Fault Record.

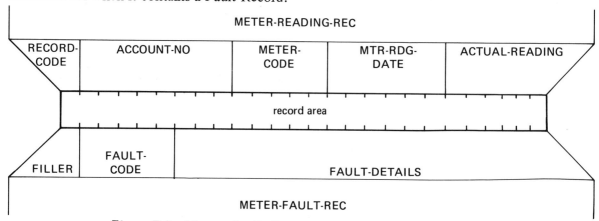

Figure 5.3   Alternative Definitions for a Single Record Area

* Strictly speaking this statement is not always true. Space for more records is sometimes allocated for efficiency reasons but the programmer can still only access the last record read.

Figure 5.4 shows the situation in which a Meter Reading Record has just been read. When the records are mixed randomly on the file the program won't know which type of record has been read. So the data-name RECORD-CODE is used to examine the first character of the record. Since it is an "R" the definition for METER-READING-REC is used to process the record. ACCOUNT-NO can be used for the Account Number (characters 2 to 9 inclusive) and so on. If FAULT-CODE is erroneously referred to, characters 2 to 6 inclusively will be accessed — the first 5 characters of the Account-No. No Fault Code is available in these locations regardless of how many Fault Records have previously been read.

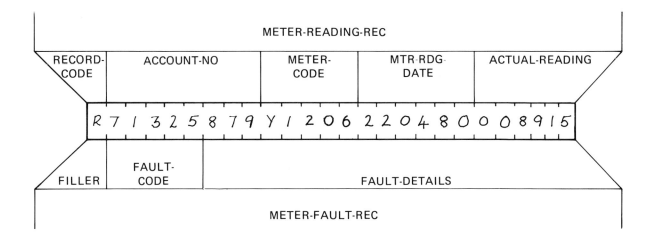

Figure 5.4   Processing a Meter Reading Record

Figure 5.5 shows the situation after reading a Fault Record. Again the program uses REC-ORD-CODE to discover what type of record has been read. Upon discovering a Fault Record only the data-names FAULT-CODE and FAULT-DETAILS would be used. The area no longer contains an Account Number, Meter Code, etc, so it would be incorrect to use ACCOUNT-NO, METER-CODE, etc. If you wish to, you could have defined a name in place of the FILLER at the start of the Fault Record. Since it would refer to the same data item as RECORD-CODE nothing is achieved by so doing.

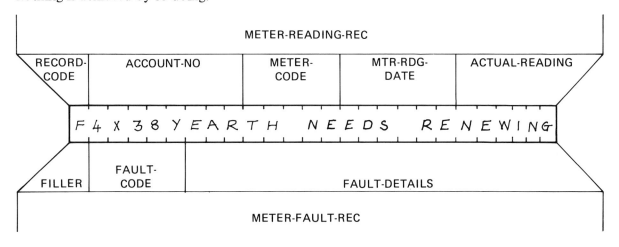

Figure 5.5   Processing a Fault Record

So, to summarise, you can have any number of record definitions following a file descript-ion entry. It is the programmer's responsibility to reference only the description of the current record. A record can no longer be accessed once another record has been read from the same file. If any record is needed for reference later on, it must be moved into the Working Storage Section (this is our next topic for discussion).

Similar principles apply to output files. You can have many record definitions but once you have written a record you can no longer access it.

5.2   THE WORKING STORAGE SECTION

Having taken care of the definition of the Fault Record, we now move on to the next program enhancement — namely the Report Heading. This is to take the form of the words READING DATES starting in the sixth position of the printline. The Report Heading can be defined as a record as shown in figure 5.6.

```
1    REPORT-HEADING.
   3 FILLER            PIC X(5)
                          VALUE SPACES.
   3 FILLER            PIC X(13)
                          VALUE "READING DATES".
   3 FILLER            PIC X(114)
                          VALUE SPACES.
```

Figure 5.6   Definition of Report Heading

You will notice that a new clause, the VALUE clause, has been used here. This is used to specify the data which you wish to be stored in a data item before the program begins execution. Having stored it, the data remains unaltered unless and until the program stores something else on top of it (by a MOVE statement for example). In this example the contents will remain unaltered throughout the running of the program.

The VALUE clause takes the form

<u>VALUE</u> IS literal

with the literal being numeric when the clause is used with numeric data items and being non-numeric for alphanumeric data items. The effect is the same as moving the literal into the data item.

There is an important restriction with VALUE. It cannot be used in the File Section. There-fore this record must be defined in the second of our Data Division Sections — The Working Stor-age Section. This is reserved for data items which have constant values or which are not input from or output to a file. The full Working Storage Section for this program is shown in figure 5.7.

In it you will notice that we have also defined the Report Footing. Unlike consecutive rec-ords in the File Section REPORT-FOOTING occupies a different storage location from REPORT-HEADING. Apart from this difference and the VALUE clause, the rules for defining records in the two Sections are the same.

All we need to do with the Report Heading is to print it at the beginning of the program. The Report Footing is printed at the end of the program. But to get the correct contents we must add 1 to READING-COUNT for every reading and add 1 to RECORD-COUNT for every record. Also we must not forget to zeroise both data items at the beginning of the program.

```
        WORKING-STORAGE SECTION.
    1        END-OF-FILE-FLAG PIC X.

    1        REPORT-HEADING.
        3    FILLER               PIC X(5)
                                  VALUE SPACES.
        3    FILLER               PIC X(13)
                                  VALUE "READING DATES".
        3    FILLER               PIC X(114)
                                  VALUE SPACES.
    1        REPORT FOOTING.
        3    FILLER               PIC X(5)
                                  VALUE SPACES.
        3    FILLER               PIC X(18)
                                  VALUE "NO. OF READINGS = ".
        3    READING-COUNT        PIC 9(4).
        3    FILLER               PIC X(5)
                                  VALUE SPACES.
        3    FILLER               PIC X(17)
                                  VALUE "NO. OF RECORDS = ".
        3    RECORD-COUNT         PIC 9(4).
        3    FILLER               PIC X(79)
                                  VALUE SPACES.
```

Figure 5.7   The Working Storage Section

5.3   THE PROCEDURE DIVISION STRUCTURE

We will now look at the Procedure Division needed for our enhanced program. We have to perform the following tasks.

Initial Processing   : Open the files and read record

Zeroise reading count and record count

Print the report heading and a blank line

Process Records   : For each record : Add 1 to record count

For each reading : Add 1 to reading count

Set up print line

Write print line

Read next record

Terminal Processing: Print blank line and report footing

Close files

Stop run

The Initial Processing is shown in figure 5.8. It is made up of statements with which we are already familiar. You will notice that, to improve readability, the initial processing has been coded as separate routines, each preceded by a comment which describes its function. The first routine "open files" consists of open statements and code closely associated with the opening of the file, and so on.

```
*open files
      OPEN INPUT METER-READINGS
      MOVE "N" TO END-OF-FILE-FLAG
      READ METER-READINGS
         AT END MOVE "Y" TO END-OF-FILE-FLAG
      END-READ
      OPEN OUTPUT METER-LIST
*zeroise totals
      MOVE 0 TO READING-COUNT RECORD-COUNT

*print heading
      MOVE REPORT-HEADING TO PRINTLINE
      WRITE PRINTLINE
      MOVE SPACES TO PRINTLINE
      WRITE PRINTLINE
```

Figure 5.8   The Initial Processing

The Terminal Processing is also made up of COBOL statements with which you are already familiar (see figure 5.9).

```
*print footing
      MOVE SPACES TO PRINTLINE
      WRITE PRINTLINE
      MOVE REPORT-FOOTING TO PRINTLINE
      WRITE PRINTLINE

*close files
      CLOSE METER-READINGS METER-LIST
      STOP RUN.
```

Figure 5.9   The Terminal Processing

You will have noticed that the heading line and the footing line were each defined to be the exact length of the Printline. In fact the trailing spaces could have been omitted since the MOVE would have achieved the desired effect for us. When data is moved to an alphanumeric data item the leftmost character is moved to the leftmost position in the receiving data item, the next character is moved to the next position and so on. If any characters don't fit they are simply omitted. If on the other hand there is any space left at the end of the field it is space filled. For example

MOVE "ANE196M" TO NO-PLATE

has the following effect

Picture of NO-PLATE	Contents of NO-PLATE after MOVE
XXX	A N E
X(10)	A N E 1 9 6 M

In the second example the spaces will be stored at the end of NO-PLATE regardless of its original contents.

When data is moved into a numeric data item the rules of alignment and padding are different. These rules are explained later.

Returning to our program, the processing of the individual records does require new COBOL statements (see figure 5.10). We need the ADD statement to increment the two counts and the IF statement to distinguish the Meter Reading Records from the Fault Records.

```
*process records
      PERFORM UNTIL END-OF-FILE-FLAG = "Y"
           ADD 1 TO RECORD-COUNT
           IF RECORD-CODE = "R"
           THEN
                ADD 1 TO READING-COUNT
                MOVE SPACES TO PRINTLINE
                MOVE METER-CODE OF METER-READING-REC
                   TO METER-CODE OF PRINTLINE
                MOVE MTR-RDG-DAY TO PL-DAY
                MOVE MTR-RDG-MONTH TO PL-MONTH
                WRITE PRINTLINE
           END-IF
           READ METER-READINGS
             AT END MOVE "Y" TO END-OF-FILE-FLAG
           END-READ
      END-PERFORM
```

Figure 5.10   The Record Processing Paragraph

In its simplest form the ADD statement consists of

$$\underline{ADD} \quad \left\{ \begin{array}{l} \text{numeric-literal} \\ \text{identifier-1} \end{array} \right\} \quad \underline{TO}\ \text{identifier-2}$$

where identifier-1 and identifier-2 both refer to numeric data items. The effect of the statement is to add the value of the numeric literal or the contents of identifier-1 to the contents of identifier-2.

So in our example:

```
ADD 1 TO RECORD-COUNT
```

would cause 1 to be added to the contents of RECORD-COUNT every time the statement is executed.

The IF statement is used whenever we wish to evaluate a condition to determine which action is appropriate. Its simplest format is

IF value-1 = value-2

    THEN statement ...

END-IF

Note that the symbol "=" must have spaces on either side of it. If value-1 does equal value-2 (in other words the condition is true) then the embedded statements (those following THEN) are executed before proceeding to the next statement, after END-IF. If the condition is false (value-1 ≠ value-2) then the computer proceeds directly to the statement after END-IF.

In the example in figure 5.10 all the coding from ADD 1 TO READING-COUNT to WRITE PRINTLINE is executed if and only if RECORD-CODE contains "R".

In the format above, each of value-1 and value-2 may be an identifier or a literal. Other types of condition may be specified in an IF statement but we will look at these later.

5.4   SAMPLE PROGRAM

Listed below is the complete program that we have built up during this chapter. A sample output is shown in figure 5.1.

```
 1       IDENTIFICATION DIVISION.
 2       PROGRAM-ID. SELECT-METER-RDGS-PROGRAM.
 3      *Author.
 4      *    J. M. TRIANCE.
 5      *Function.
 6      *    This program reads a file of meter readings
 7      *    and fault records. It
 8      *      - lists the meter code, day and month of
 9      *        the readings
10      *      - prints the total number of reading
11      *        records and records of either type.
12
13       ENVIRONMENT DIVISION.
14       CONFIGURATION SECTION.
15       SOURCE-COMPUTER. ANS-2000.
16       OBJECT-COMPUTER. ANS-2000.
17
18       INPUT-OUTPUT SECTION.
19       FILE-CONTROL.
20           SELECT METER-READINGS ASSIGN TO MTRS35.
21           SELECT METER-LIST ASSIGN TO MTRL25.
22
23       DATA DIVISION.
24       FILE SECTION.
25       FD      METER-READINGS LABEL RECORDS STANDARD.
26       1       METER-READING-REC.
27         3     RECORD-CODE        PIC X.
28         3     ACCOUNT-NO         PIC 9(8).
29         3     METER-CODE         PIC X(5).
30         3     MTR-RDG-DATE.
31           5 MTR-RDG-DAY        PIC 99.
32           5 MTR-RDG-MONTH      PIC 99.
33           5 MTR-RDG-YEAR       PIC 99.
34         3     ACTUAL-READING     PIC 9(6).
35       1       METER-FAULT-REC.
36         3     FILLER             PIC X.
37         3     FAULT-CODE         PIC X(5).
38         3     FAULT-DETAILS      PIC X(20).
39       FD      METER-LIST LABEL RECORDS OMITTED.
40       1       PRINTLINE.
41         3     FILLER             PIC X(10).
42         3     METER-CODE         PIC X(5).
43         3     FILLER             PIC X(5).
44         3     PL-DATE.
45           5 PL-DAY             PIC X(2).
46           5 FILLER             PIC X.
47           5 PL-MONTH           PIC X(2).
48         3     FILLER             PIC X(107).
49
50       WORKING-STORAGE SECTION.
51       1       END-OF-FILE-FLAG PIC X.
52
53       1       REPORT-HEADING.
```

```
54        3    FILLER              PIC X(5)
55                                    VALUE SPACES.
56        3    FILLER              PIC X(13)
57                                    VALUE "READING DATES".
58        3    FILLER              PIC X(114)
59                                    VALUE SPACES.
60     1     REPORT-FOOTING.
61        3    FILLER              PIC X(5)
62                                    VALUE SPACES.
63        3    FILLER              PIC X(18)
64                                    VALUE "NO. OF READINGS = ".
65        3    READING-COUNT       PIC 9(4).
66        3    FILLER              PIC X(5)
67                                    VALUE SPACES.
68        3    FILLER              PIC X(17)
69                                    VALUE "NO. OF RECORDS = ".
70        3    RECORD-COUNT        PIC 9(4).
71        3    FILLER              PIC X(79)
72                                    VALUE SPACES.
73
74     PROCEDURE DIVISION.
75     SELECT-METER-READINGS.
76
77  *open files
78        OPEN INPUT METER-READINGS
70        MOVE "N" TO END-OF-FILE-FLAG
80        READ METER-READINGS
81          AT END MOVE "Y" TO END-OF-FILE-FLAG
82        END-READ
83        OPEN OUTPUT METER-LIST
84
85  *zeroise totals
86        MOVE 0 TO READING-COUNT RECORD-COUNT
87
88  *print heading
89        MOVE REPORT-HEADING TO PRINTLINE
90        WRITE PRINTLINE
91        MOVE SPACES TO PRINTLINE
92        WRITE PRINTLINE
93
94  *process records
95        PERFORM UNTIL END-OF-FILE-FLAG = "Y"
96             ADD 1 TO RECORD-COUNT
97             IF RECORD-CODE = "R"
98             THEN
99                 ADD 1 TO READING-COUNT
100                MOVE SPACES TO PRINTLINE
101                MOVE METER-CODE OF METER-READING-REC
102                   TO METER-CODE OF PRINTLINE
103                MOVE MTR-RDG-DAY TO PL-DAY
104                MOVE MTR-RDG-MONTH TO PL-MONTH
105                WRITE PRINTLINE
106            END-IF
107            READ METER-READINGS
108              AT END MOVE "Y" TO END-OF-FILE-FLAG
109            END-READ
110        END-PERFORM
111
```

```
112     *print footing
113          MOVE SPACES TO PRINTLINE
114          WRITE PRINTLINE
115          MOVE REPORT-FOOTING TO PRINTLINE
116          WRITE PRINTLINE
117
118     *close files
119          CLOSE METER-READINGS METER-LIST
120          STOP RUN.
```

5.5 SUMMARY

This chapter introduced some new elements of COBOL which will be used in most COBOL programs you write. They are

Records with different formats on the same file

The Working Storage Section

Moving data between alphanumeric data items of different lengths

The ADD statement

The IF statement

There is more to Arithmetic than the ADD statement we used and there is more to learn about the IF statement. There is also more to learn about report production: for example we should really print the heading at the top of each page and we should remove the leading zeros from the Reading Count and Record Count when we print them. These topics will be covered in the next few chapters.

QUIZ

1.   Study the following definitions

```
FD  ACCOUNTS  LABEL RECORDS STANDARD
               DATA RECORDS DEBIT CREDIT.
1   DEBIT.
 3  RECORD-CODE   PIC 9.
 3  DB-DATE       PIC 9(6).
 3  DB-VALUE      PIC 9(5).
 3  DB-INVOICE-NO PIC X(7).
1   CREDIT.
 3  FILLER        PIC 9.
 3  PAYMENT-TYPE  PIC X.
 3  CR-DATE       PIC 9(6).
 3  CR-VALUE      PIC 9(7).
 3  CR-NUMBER     PIC 9(4).
```

(a)   How many characters of storage are reserved, in total, for these two definitions?

(b)   How can the data in the field described as FILLER be accessed?

(c)   What happens if a DEBIT record is read and then the data item PAYMENT-TYPE is accessed?

2.   Which of the following VALUE clauses are valid?

(a)   PIC X(4) VALUE 9000.

(b)   PIC X(4) VALUE "9.36".

(c)   PIC 999 VALUE SPACES.

(d)   1 OLDEST-DATE   VALUE 7001.
        3 OLDEST-YEAR   PIC 99.
        3 OLDEST-MONTH PIC 99.

(e)   PIC X(5) VALUE ZEROS.

(f)   PIC X(5) VALUE SPACE.

3.   Rewrite the following as one COBOL statement

          MOVE REPORT-HEADING TO PRINTLINE

          WRITE PRINTLINE

      (Hint: refer to rules for WRITE in the *Reference Summary*.)

4.   Write down the coding to add 1 to DEBIT-COUNT if the data item RECORD-CODE con-
      tains 1 and then in all cases add 1 to RECORD-COUNT.

OTHER FEATURES

When you write your own programs you will submit them to a COBOL compiler which will in-
form you if you have broken any rules of COBOL. When these errors have been corrected you
will be able to test your programs — run them with sample data and check that they produce the
correct results.

When the wrong results are produced it will be necessary to debug the program — locate the
program error and correct it. This is not always an easy task.

Some computers provide special debugging software packages which do such things as

   —   output the paragraph-name as each paragraph is executed

   —   output the contents of specified data items every time they are referenced or every
        time they are changed.

Such information can help you localise and then detect the error.

If debugging software is not available you can achieve the same effect for yourself using the
DISPLAY statement and D lines.

1.   The DISPLAY Statement

DISPLAY is a convenient way of outputting debugging information to a printer or visual display
unit. You can for example write

          DISPLAY "RECORD CODE = " RECORD-CODE

to display on the compiler's standard output device the message in quotation marks followed by
the contents of RECORD-CODE. So if RECORD-CODE contains F the above DISPLAY statement would output:

          RECORD CODE = F

If this statement appeared immediately after the READ in the program in section 5.4 you would be able to trace the progress of the program through the input file.

Any mixture of literals and identifiers may appear in a DISPLAY statement. It is also possible to indicate a different output device using the UPON phrase.

2. D-Lines and WITH DEBUGGING MODE

Any lines which are specifically for debugging may be written with a D in the indicator area. Suppose that a data item PL-MONTH sometimes has spaces erroneously stored in it and we wish to discover why. We might insert the following debugging code:

I	area A	area B
		MOVE CALCULATED-MONTH TO PL-MONTH
D		IF PL-MONTH = SPACES
D		DISPLAY "PL-MONTH = " PL-MONTH
D		"CALCULATED-MONTH = " CALCULATED-MONTH
		WRITE PRINTLINE

If you put D in the indicator area you then have the option of telling the compiler to accept that line as normal coding or treat it as comments. If you specify WITH DEBUGGING MODE in the source computer paragraph all the coding with D in the indicator area will be compiled normally (as if the D had been omitted). If the WITH DEBUGGING MODE is not specified the coding with D in the indicator area will be treated as comments (as if an asterisk had been written instead of D).

If WITH DEBUGGING MODE is specified you still have the option at run time of indicating whether or not you want the D-lines to be executed.

Thus you can have debugging lines in your program which you execute only when you need the extra information they provide. Then when you have finished testing you can recompile the program without the D-lines simply by removing the WITH DEBUGGING MODE clause.

3. The JUSTIFIED Clause

The normal alignment rules for alphanumeric data items can be over-ruled. Instead of aligning the leftmost character with the leftmost position of the receiving item we can force the compiler to align the rightmost character with the rightmost position. This is achieved by writing

    JUSTIFIED RIGHT

in the data description entry of the receiving data item. When there are any lefthand characters which don't fit they are truncated and when there are unused spaces in the receiving item they are space filled. If the sending and receiving items are the same length the JUSTIFIED clause has no effect.

6 Procedure Division Structure

When you come to write larger programs it is important that anyone reading them will find them easy to understand. You will need to understand how they work when you come to debug them — it is surprising how quickly you can forget what the function of a piece of coding is, especially in a large program. A bigger problem is for some other programmer who has to amend your program months or years after you have written it. Most COBOL programs are run repeatedly over a period of some years and during that time the specifications will invariably be changed — thus necessitating a change to the program.

The part of the COBOL program which is liable to present most problems of understanding is the Procedure Division. One of the most important aids to Procedure Division readability is to divide it into smaller units each of which can be more easily understood. In the programs so far, we achieved this by writing each of them as one paragraph divided into a number of smaller routines headed by comments. It is however unusual for programs to consist of only one paragraph. We will see how paragraphs are used to improve readability in larger programs.

6.1 A VALIDATION PROGRAM

To illustrate the use of paragraphs we will look at a simple validation program. The program is required to read a file of meter readings — like the one we first came across. The program must check that the account number and reading are numeric and the date is valid. Each valid record is copied to a disk file and every time an error is found a message is printed.

Before we get involved in the detail we will look at the overall structure of the program. We will have a control paragraph which ensures that the major functions in the program are controlled in the correct sequence and the correct number of times. An outline of this paragraph appears in Figure 6.1.

```
MAIN-CONTROL.
        do initial-processing
        for each record
            do record processing
        do terminal-processing
        STOP RUN
```

Figure 6.1 Structure of MAIN-CONTROL Section

The words written in lower case in this figure still have to be expressed in COBOL.

59

6.2   THE OUT-OF-LINE PERFORM STATEMENT

The MAIN-CONTROL paragraph gives a clear statement of the major tasks performed by the program — it thus would be a mistake to clutter it up with the lower level of detail in the program. To avoid this we can program the other main functions (Initial-processing, Record Processing and Terminal-processing) in other paragraphs and indicate in the MAIN-CONTROL paragraph the points at which they are to be executed. This is done by use of the out-of-line PERFORM statement as illustrated in figure 6.2. The basic format of this statement is

    PERFORM paragraph-name

The effect of this statement is to execute the whole of the paragraph identified by paragraph-name.

Execution always begins at the start of the Procedure Division. So, in figure 6.2, PERFORM INITIAL-PROCESSING is the first statement executed. This causes the whole of the INITIAL-PROCESSING paragraph to be executed (up to but excluding the next paragraph-name, PROCESS-RECORD). The computer then executes the next statement after PERFORM INITIAL-PROCESSING (ie PERFORM PROCESS-RECORD), and so on.

(When you come to look at the full format of PERFORM you will see that it starts

    PERFORM procedure-name ...

A paragraph-name is one of two kinds of procedure-name. For the time being it is best to regard procedure-name as synonymous with paragraph-name.)

```
PROCEDURE DIVISION.
MAIN-CONTROL.
    PERFORM INITIAL-PROCESSING
    PERFORM PROCESS-RECORD
    PERFORM TERMINAL-PROCESSING
    STOP RUN.

INITIAL-PROCESSING.
    OPEN INPUT METER-READINGS
    MOVE "N" TO END-OF-INPUT-FLAG
    READ METER-READINGS
        AT END MOVE "Y" TO END-OF-INPUT-FLAG
    END-READ
    OPEN OUTPUT VALID-READINGS
                    ERROR-LISTING.

PROCESS-RECORD.
    :
    :

TERMINAL-PROCESSING.
    :
    :
```

Figure 6.2 The Out-of-Line PERFORM Statement in Use

Let us now look at the statement following PERFORM INITIAL-PROCESSING. We need here to keep performing PROCESS-RECORD paragraph as long as there are any records to process. We see from the INITIAL-PROCESSING paragraph that "N" (short for no) has been stored in END-OF-INPUT-FLAG and "Y" (short for yes) will be moved to it when we reach the end of the file. So we need to continually perform PROCESS-RECORD until END-OF-INPUT-FLAG is equal to "Y". We can, in fact, write it in COBOL just like that:

```
PERFORM PROCESS-RECORD
    UNTIL END-OF-INPUT-FLAG = "Y"
```

This has some similarities to the in-line PERFORM statement used in Chapter 4. In fact the coding

```
PERFORM UNTIL END-OF-INPUT-FLAG = "Y"
statements to process 1 record
END-PERFORM
```

produces the same effect as

```
PERFORM PROCESS-RECORD
    UNTIL END-OF-INPUT-FLAG = "Y"
            .
            .
            .

PROCESS-RECORD.
    statements to process 1 record.
```

The difference is entirely one of program readability. If you think that the code is clearer if you have the record processing statements with the PERFORM statement, you use the in-line PERFORM. If, on the other hand, you think that the record processing statements are too detailed for that part of the program you place them elsewhere in the program and use the out-of-line PERFORM statement.

In the paragraph PROCESS-RECORD, coding must be written to (i) validate each of the data items (except for the METER-CODE which can take any value), (ii) write a record to VALID-READINGS if there are no errors, (iii) read the next record.

The same argument applies to this paragraph as did to the main control paragraph — if all the detailed coding appeared in the paragraph the structure would become obscure. Thus the main functions are coded in separated paragraphs and are performed (see figure 6.3).

```
PROCESS-RECORD.
    MOVE ZERO TO ERROR-COUNT
    MOVE SPACES TO PRINTLINE
    PERFORM ACCOUNT-NO-CHECK
    PERFORM DATE-CHECK
    PERFORM READING-CHECK
    IF NO-ERRORS
    THEN
            MOVE METER-READING-REC TO VALID-RECORD
            WRITE VALID-RECORD
    END-IF
    READ METER-READINGS
    AT END MOVE "Y" TO END-OF-INPUT-FLAG
    END-READ.
```

Figure 6.3 PROCESS-RECORD Paragraph

A common way of documenting the structure of a program is by means of a module hierarchy chart.

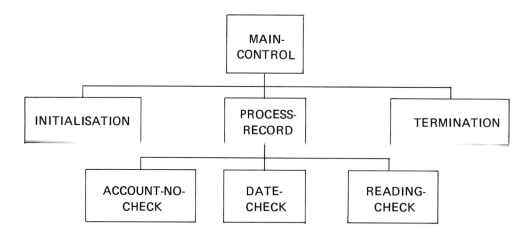

Figure 6.4 Module Hierarchy Chart for Validate Program

In figure 6.4 each box corresponds to one paragraph in the Procedure Division. Where two boxes are linked together it implies the upper one performs the lower one. As can be seen a performed paragraph can itself perform other paragraphs. These, in turn, can perform other paragraphs and so on. The only restriction is that no paragraph is allowed to perform itself either directly or indirectly. The implication of this diagram is that the lines joining the boxes represent the only links between the paragraphs — this results in a clean and easily understood structure.

6.3 CONDITIONS

Conditions are tested in the Procedure Division to determine which of two possible actions is to be executed next. We have already encountered some: RECORD-CODE = "R" in the last chapter, and END-OF-INPUT-FLAG = "Y" in the PERFORM UNTIL statement. These are examples of relation conditions. We will look at these along with the other commonly used types of COBOL condition.

6.3.1   Relation Conditions

The general form of a relation condition is

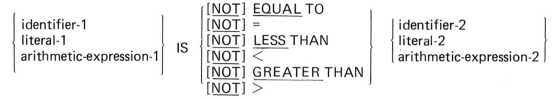

So examples of relation conditions are

ERROR–COUNT = 0

ERROR–COUNT EQUAL TO ZERO

ERROR–COUNT IS > 0

RECORD–CODE < EXCEPTION–CODE

3 IS NOT LESS THAN LINE–COUNT

The meaning of these is obvious. Arithmetic expressions, which may be used on either side of the condition, will be discussed in the next chapter.

6.3.2 Class Conditions

This condition is used to test whether a data item is numeric or whether it is alphabetic. Its format is

$$\text{identifier IS [\underline{NOT}]} \quad \left\{ \begin{array}{l} \underline{\text{NUMERIC}} \\ \underline{\text{ALPHABETIC}} \end{array} \right\}$$

The condition ACCOUNT-NO IS NUMERIC is , for example, true if ACCOUNT-NO consists entirely of numeric digits. ADDRESS IS ALPHABETIC is true if ADDRESS consists entirely of letters of the alphabet and spaces. The NOT, of course, simply reverses the value of the condition.

6.3.3 Condition-name Conditions

With an elementary item it is possible to give names to the various values that the data item might contain. In figure 6.5, for example, the value "D" in ACCOUNT-TYPE is given the name DOMESTIC, "F" is given the name FARM, and BUSINESS applies to both values "F" and "T".

```
3      ACCOUNT-TYPE  PIC X.
   88   DOMESTIC      VALUE "D".
   88   FARM          VALUE "F".
   88   BUSINESS      VALUE "F" "T".
```

Figure 6.5 Definition of Condition-names

The names, known as *condition-names*, are defined by using a special level number 88, immediately after the relevant data item.

These condition-names can be used in the Procedure Division. For example, instead of writing

```
IF ACCOUNT-TYPE = "D"
```

we can write

```
IF DOMESTIC
```

We can write

```
IF FARM
```

to test whether ACCOUNT-TYPE contains "F", and we can write

```
IF BUSINESS
```

to test whether ACCOUNT-TYPE contains "F" or "T": BUSINESS is true if ACCOUNT-TYPE contains "F" or if it contains "T".

The word NOT can be placed in front of any condition-name to test the opposite condition. Thus

```
IF NOT DOMESTIC
```

is the same as

```
IF ACCOUNT-TYPE NOT = "D"
```

6.3.4   Combined Conditions

The three types of condition described above are examples of what are known as *simple conditions*. Each of these can be combined with other simple conditions to make *combined conditions*.

For example we can write

```
IF BALANCE < LIMIT
    AND DOMESTIC
```

This condition is true only if both simple conditions are true; that is BALANCE is less than LIMIT, and DOMESTIC is true (ie ACCOUNT-TYPE = "D" in the example in the previous section).

We can also write

```
IF ACCOUNT-TYPE = "F"
    OR ACCOUNT-TYPE = "T"
```

This condition is true if either one (or both) of the simple conditions is true. It is thus equivalent to writing

```
IF BUSINESS
```

using the above definition of BUSINESS.

6.4   THE IF STATEMENT

All the conditions described above can be used in the UNTIL option of the PERFORM statement.

The conditions can also be used in the IF statement whose format is

IF condition
THEN statement-1 ...
ELSE statement-2 ...
END-IF

If "condition" is true then statement-1 is executed before proceeding to the next statement. If "condition" is false and ELSE is specified then statement-2 is executed before proceeding to the next statement. As we saw in the last chapter if "condition" is false and no ELSE clause is specified, control is handed directly to the next statement.

For example we can write

```
IF CURRENT < ZERO
THEN
    PERFORM CHECK-DEPOSIT
ELSE
    PERFORM GIVE-INTEREST
END-IF
```

In this example the statement PERFORM CHECK-DEPOSIT is executed if CURRENT is less than zero, otherwise PERFORM GIVE-INTEREST is executed. In both cases the READ statement is executed after the appropriate PERFORM.

In the format for IF, statement-1 and statement-2 may be repeated. We may, for example, write

```
IF   MTR-RDG-DATE NUMERIC
THEN
     PERFORM DAY-CHECK
     PERFORM MONTH-CHECK
     PERFORM YEAR-CHECK
ELSE
     MOVE "DATE NOT NUMERIC" TO PL-MESSAGE
     PERFORM PRINT-MESSAGE
END-IF
```

All the statements between the words THEN and ELSE are executed if the condition is true. All the statements between ELSE and END-IF are executed if the condition is not true.

Note that the statements making up statement-1... and statement-2... have been indented. This is an almost universal convention for emphasising the structure of the coding. Even if the IF statement spreads over many lines the associated ELSE and END-IF can be located at a glance.

Any statement in either of these strings of statements (or the only statement when there is only one) may be another IF statement (see figure 6.6).

```
IF   MTR-RDG-DATE NUMERIC
THEN
     PERFORM DAY-CHECK
     IF MONTH < 1 OR MONTH > 12
     THEN
          MOVE "N" TO DATE-OK-FLAG
     ELSE
          MOVE "Y" TO DATE-OK-FLAG
     END-IF
     PERFORM YEAR-CHECK
ELSE
     MOVE "DATE NOT NUMERIC" TO PL-MESSAGE
     PERFORM PRINT-MESSAGE
END-IF
```

Figure 6.6 A Nested IF Statement

The nested IF statement is just like any other statement: after execution it proceeds to the next statement. So if MTR-RDG-DATE is numeric, PERFORM DAY-CHECK is executed, followed by MOVE "N" to DATE-OK-FLAG or MOVE "Y" to DATE-OK-FLAG depending on whether or not

MONTH < 1 or MONTH > 12

is true, followed by PERFORM YEAR-CHECK. Take care not to miss off any END-IFs – this could alter the meaning of your code or make it unacceptable to the compiler.

Note that although the coding in figure 6.6 is perfectly legal it could be criticised on the grounds of its style. It is inconsistent to expand the routine for checking the month in-line but leave the day and year checking routines out-of-line.

6.5 THE CONTINUE STATEMENT

The format of the IF statement

IF condition
THEN statement-1 ...
[ELSE statement-2 ...]
END-IF

permits the ELSE phrase to be omitted if no action is required when the condition is false.

However statement-1 must always be specified even if no action is to be taken when the condition is true. In these circumstances the CONTINUE statement can be used — it is a special statement which does nothing.

Thus you can write

```
IF   AGE > 25 AND CLAIMS = 0
THEN
      CONTINUE
ELSE
      PERFORM REVIEW-PREMIUM
END-IF
```

The action of this statement is to do nothing if the condition is true (AGE is greater than 25 and CLAIMS is zero). Otherwise PERFORM REVIEW-PREMIUM.

The use of CONTINUE could be avoided by twisting the statement round:

```
IF   AGE NOT > 25 OR CLAIMS NOT = 0
THEN
      PERFORM REVIEW-PREMIUM
END-IF
```

However, it's often better to use CONTINUE rather than contort the conditions since this can lead to errors or a condition which is harder to understand.

6.6 THE EVALUATE STATEMENT

When the action taken depends on some condition, we have so far used the IF statement. The IF statement is however designed for only two alternatives — when there are more the EVALUATE statement will be used. An example of the Evaluate statement is given in figure 6.7.

```
EVALUATE TRUE
WHEN DISCOUNT-CODE = 1 MOVE 7 TO DISCOUNT-RATE
WHEN DISCOUNT-CODE = 2 MOVE 10 TO DISCOUNT-RATE
WHEN DISCOUNT-CODE = 3 MOVE 15 TO DISCOUNT-RATE
OTHERWISE PERFORM INVALID-DISCOUNT
END-EVALUATE
```

Figure 6.7 An EVALUATE Statement

When this statement is executed, each condition is tested in turn. The statement (or statements) following the first true condition is executed before proceeding to the statement after END-EVALUATE. If no conditions are true the statement (or statements) following OTHERWISE are executed.

Thus the effect of the statement in figure 6.7 is to execute

```
    MOVE  7 TO DISCOUNT-RATE if DISCOUNT-CODE is 1,
    MOVE 10 TO DISCOUNT-RATE if DISCOUNT-CODE is 2,
    MOVE 15 TO DISCOUNT-RATE if DISCOUNT-CODE is 3
and PERFORM INVALID-DISCOUNT otherwise.
```

The condition that follows WHEN may be any COBOL condition, and a string of statements may follow the condition.

The Evaluate statement may take a number of different forms. One of the most useful ones can be used when various conditions have the same subject; thus the example in figure 6.7 can be written as follows:

```
EVALUATE DISCOUNT-CODE
WHEN 1 MOVE  7 TO DISCOUNT-RATE
WHEN 2 MOVE 10 TO DISCOUNT-RATE
WHEN 3 MOVE 15 TO DISCOUNT-RATE
OTHERWISE PERFORM INVALID-DISCOUNT
END-EVALUATE
```

6.7 SAMPLE PROGRAM

Listed below is a sample program showing how a Procedure Division can be constructed of paragraphs linked by PERFORMs. It also shows some examples of the IF statements discussed in this chapter.

```
1     IDENTIFICATION DIVISION.
2     PROGRAM-ID. VALIDATE-METER-RDGS-PROGRAM.
3    *Author. J M Triance.
4    *Function.
5    *    This program demonstrates the use of procedure division
6    *    sections, perform and if. The program reads in a file
7    *    and prints all invalid records giving an appropriate error
8    *    message, and produces a file with all the valid records.
9    *Limitation.
10   *    The program does not yet produce page headings.
11
12    ENVIRONMENT DIVISION.
13    CONFIGURATION SECTION.
14    SOURCE-COMPUTER. ANS-2000.
15    OBJECT-COMPUTER. ANS-2000.
16
17    INPUT-OUTPUT SECTION.
18    FILE-CONTROL.
19        SELECT METER-READINGS ASSIGN MTRS36.
20        SELECT VALID-READINGS ASSIGN MTRVAL.
21        SELECT ERROR-LISTING ASSIGN MOUTPUT.
22
23    DATA DIVISION.
24    FILE SECTION.
25    FD    METER-READINGS        LABEL RECORD OMITTED.
26    1     METER-READING-REC.
27      3     RECORD-CODE           PIC X.
```

```
28        3        ACCOUNT-NO              PIC 9(8).
29        3        METER-CODE              PIC X(5).
30        3        MTR-RDG-DATE.
31          5      MTR-RDG-DAY             PIC 99.
32          88 DAY-IN-RANGE                            VALUE 1 THRU 31.
33          5      MTR-RDG-MONTH           PIC 99.
34          88 MONTH-IN-RANGE                          VALUE 1 THRU 12.
35          5      MTR-RDG-YEAR            PIC 99.
36          88 YEAR-IN-RANGE                           VALUE 81 THRU 99.
37        3        ACTUAL-READING          PIC 9(6).
38
39   FD        VALID-READINGS             LABEL RECORD STANDARD.
40   1         VALID-RECORD               PIC X(26).
41
42   FD        ERROR-LISTING              LABEL RECORD OMITTED.
43   1         PRINTLINE.
44        3        FILLER                 PIC X(10).
45        3        PL-READING-REC         PIC X(26).
46        3        FILLER                 PIC X(5).
47        3        PL-ERROR-MESSAGE       PIC X(30).
48        3        FILLER                 PIC X(61).
49
50   WORKING-STORAGE SECTION.
51   1         END-OF-INPUT-FLAG          PIC X.
52          88 END-OF-INPUT                            VALUE "Y".
53
54   1         ERROR-COUNT                PIC 9.
55          88 NO-ERRORS                               VALUE 0.
56
57   PROCEDURE DIVISION.
58   MAIN-CONTROL.
59       PERFORM INITIAL-PROCESSING
60       PERFORM PROCESS-RECORD
61         UNTIL END-OF-INPUT
62       PERFORM TERMINAL-PROCESSING
63       STOP RUN.
64
65   INITIAL-PROCESSING.
66       OPEN INPUT  METER-READINGS
67       MOVE "N" TO END-OF-INPUT-FLAG
68       READ METER-READINGS
69         AT END MOVE "Y" TO END-OF-INPUT-FLAG
70       END-READ
71       OPEN OUTPUT VALID-READINGS
72                   ERROR-LISTING.
73
74   PROCESS-RECORD.
75       MOVE ZERO TO ERROR-COUNT
76       MOVE SPACES TO PRINTLINE
77       PERFORM ACCOUNT-NO-CHECK
78       PERFORM DATE-CHECK
79       PERFORM READING-CHECK
80       IF NO-ERRORS
81       THEN
82           MOVE METER-READING-REC TO VALID-RECORD
83           WRITE VALID-RECORD
84       END-IF
```

```
 85              READ METER-READINGS
 86              AT END MOVE "Y" TO END-OF-INPUT-FLAG
 87              END-READ.
 88
 89          TERMINAL-PROCESSING.
 90              CLOSE METER-READINGS VALID-READINGS ERROR-LISTING.
 91
 92          ACCOUNT-NO-CHECK.
 93      *       The validation of account number
 94      *       should be coded here.
 95
 96          DATE-CHECK.
 97      *       This is a simplified validation of the date.
 98              IF MTR-RDG-DATE NUMERIC
 99              THEN
100                  IF      DAY-IN-RANGE
101                      AND MONTH-IN-RANGE
102                      AND YEAR-IN-RANGE
103                  THEN
104                      CONTINUE
105                  ELSE
106                      MOVE "DATE OUT OF RANGE" TO PL-ERROR-MESSAGE
107                      PERFORM PROCESS-ERROR
108                  END-IF
109              ELSE
110                  MOVE "DATE NOT NUMERIC" TO PL-ERROR-MESSAGE
111                  PERFORM PROCESS-ERROR
112              END-IF.
113
114          READING-CHECK.
115      *       The validation of actual reading
116      *       should be coded here.
117
118          PROCESS-ERROR.
119              MOVE METER-READING-REC TO PL-READING-REC
120              WRITE PRINTLINE
121                 AFTER 2 LINES
122              ADD 1 TO ERROR-COUNT.
```

6.8 SUMMARY

The following have been covered in this chapter

PERFORM paragraph-name [UNTIL condition]

IF condition
THEN statement-1 ...
[ELSE statement-2 ...]
END-IF

relation conditions:

[NOT] =, [NOT] >, [NOT] < and equivalents in words

class conditions:

> NUMERIC and ALPHABETIC

condition-name conditions

> level 88 entries

combined conditions

CONTINUE statement

EVALUATE statement

PERFORM can be used to produce well-structured programs. Within the paragraphs the use of the ELSE clause, nested IF's and combined conditions in appropriate circumstances can make the coding much more readable than has so far been possible. Condition-names can be used surprisingly frequently to remove complexity from the Procedure Division. As with all names, for best readability the condition-name should be chosen with care — to represent the condition it replaces.

QUIZ

1.   What is wrong with the following PERFORM statements?

```
COMPONENT-CHECK.
    PERFORM VALIDATE-COMP-TYPE

            •
            •
            •

VALIDATE-COMP-TYPE.
    PERFORM COMPONENT-CHECK.
```

2.   Write a statement which will cause a paragraph called REJECT-ORDER to be executed if a field QUANTITY is non-numeric.

3.   Study the following coding

```
3       BALANCE        PIC 9(5).
3       DISCOUNT-CODE  PIC X.
 88     HIGH-DISCOUNT           VALUE "H".
3       DISCOUNT       PIC 99.
            •
            •
            •
IF  HIGH-DISCOUNT
THEN
        IF  BALANCE > 500
        THEN
            MOVE 10 TO DISCOUNT
        ELSE
            MOVE 5 TO DISCOUNT
        END-IF
ELSE
        MOVE 2 TO DISCOUNT
END-IF
```

What will DISCOUNT contain if

(a)   BALANCE contains 600 and DISCOUNT-CODE contains "E"?

(b)   BALANCE contains 40 and DISCOUNT-CODE contains "H"?

4. Recode the nested IF statement in the previous question using a single EVALUATE statement.

5. Recode the following using condition-names

    ```
    3 MONTH PIC 99.
            •
            •
            •
        IF MONTH = 12
            PERFORM YEAR-END-PROCESS
        END-IF
        IF MONTH = 1
            OR MONTH = 4
            OR MONTH = 7
            OR MONTH = 10
            PERFORM QUARTERLY-PROCESS
        END-IF
        IF MONTH > 4 AND MONTH < 10
            PERFORM SEASONAL-PROCESS
        END-IF
    ```

    (Hint: for the last IF read about the THRU option of format 2 VALUE)

6. What prevents the three IF statements in the previous question being replaced by a single EVALUATE statement?

OTHER FEATURES

1. Alternative Branches

IF has an alternative branch (ie the ELSE branch) to the THEN branch. So also do all other statements which permit conditional code.

For example, a fuller format of READ is

```
READ file-name
AT END statement-1 ...
[NOT AT END statement-2 ...]
END-READ
```

The statements following AT END are executed if the READ currently being executed encounters the end of the file, otherwise the statements following NOT AT END are executed.

2. PERFORM WITH TEST AFTER

When the UNTIL option of PERFORM is used the condition is tested before each execution of the specified coding (embedded statements or the specified procedures) including the first. However, you can execute the statements or procedures once before testing the condition by using the WITH TEST AFTER option. For example

```
PERFORM PROCESS-ORDER
    WITH TEST AFTER UNTIL END-OF-FILE
```

is the same as

```
PERFORM PROCESS-ORDER
PERFORM PROCESS-ORDER UNTIL END-OF-FILE
```

It ensures the specified coding as executed at least once.

3. PERFORM THROUGH

It is possible to perform a range of paragraphs with a single PERFORM statement:

PERFORM paragraph-name-1 THROUGH paragraph-name-2

would transfer control to the start of the paragraph named paragraph-name-1 and control would return when the end of the paragraph named paragraph-name-2 was reached.

Warning: Using the THROUGH option in an undisciplined manner can cause all sorts of problems. The method of structuring shown in the body of the chapter, using PERFORM paragraph-name, is adequate for any program you will write and it avoids the pitfalls arising from this alternative approach. The alternative approach is only mentioned so that you are aware of its existence.

4. PERFORM TIMES

A special format of PERFORM is available for performing a procedure a given number of times. For example

```
PERFORM TEST-PRINT 10 TIMES
```

would execute TEST-PRINT ten times before proceeding to the statement after the PERFORM. Any integer or any identifier which refers to a data item containing an integer may be specified before the reserved word TIMES.

5. Comparing Items of Unequal Length

Items of unequal length may be compared in relation conditions. If the items are numeric there is no problem since the numeric values of the items are compared. If the items are alphanumeric the shorter item has, for the purposes of comparison, sufficient spaces added to the right hand end of it to make it the same length as the longer item.

6. Comparing Alphanumeric Items

Alphanumeric items are compared a character at a time from left to right. They are equal if all the pairs of characters are the same. If they are not equal the first pair of unequal characters determines which is larger. The item containing the larger of this pair is the larger item (that is it is GREATER THAN the other item). All the characters which a computer recognises are placed in a sequence known as the computer's *collating sequence* — each character is greater than all the characters that precede it in this sequence. The digits 0 to 9 always appear in the correct sequence as do the letters A to Z. On some computers the digits are greater than the letters and on others the digits are less than the letters. The position of other characters (space, comma, hyphen, etc) in the sequence also varies.

7. Abbreviated Combined Conditions

When the same subject appears in the consecutive relation conditions in a combined condition, the subject may be omitted from the second condition. For example

$$IF \quad AGE \; > 17$$
$$AND \quad AGE \; < 66$$

may be abbreviated to

$$IF \quad AGE \; > 17$$
$$AND \qquad < 66$$

If the subject and the relational operator are the same they may both be omitted from the second condition. For example

$$IF \quad ACCOUNT-TYPE \; = \; "F"$$
$$OR \; ACCOUNT-TYPE \; = \; "T"$$

may be abbreviated to

$$IF \; ACCOUNT-TYPE \; = \; "F" \; OR \; "T"$$

8. Sign Condition

This condition can be used to test whether a data item is positive, negative or zero. You can write

$$\underline{IF} \; identifier \; IS \; [\underline{NOT}] \; \begin{Bmatrix} \underline{POSITIVE} \\ \underline{NEGATIVE} \\ \underline{ZERO} \end{Bmatrix}$$

The same effect can be obtained using relation conditions.

9. The GO TO Statement

This statement "permanently" transfers control to another part of the program. The format is

$$\underline{GO} \; TO \; paragraph\text{-}name.$$

It causes execution of the program to proceed with the first statement in the named paragraph. Unlike PERFORM, however, there is no automatic return to the statement following the GO TO.

This is generally considered by advocates of structured programming to be an undesirable statement. Its use can make programs very difficult to understand.

7 Arithmetic in COBOL

So far the arithmetic we have used has been no more complicated than

    ADD 1 TO RECORD-COUNT

It is uncommon for COBOL programs to involve many really complex calculations but we obviously need to be able to do more than add 1 to a total. In this chapter we will look at other capabilities of ADD and we will look at the other standard arithmetic operations.

We start, however, by looking more carefully at how numbers are stored in COBOL programs.

7.1 STORAGE OF NUMBERS

In an earlier chapter we saw that we could use numeric literals such as

    480

    48.35

    -27.9

These are all values we might wish to use in a program and store in data items. The first one could be stored in a data item with PICTURE 999.

The Picture character 9 is used to describe numeric data items but by itself can only describe data items capable of containing positive integers. We need two extra picture characters to indicate the existence of a sign and a decimal point.

The picture character V is used to indicate the position of the decimal point. For example PICTURE 99V99 would be used to store four digits, the last two of which are decimal places. Thus 48.35 would be stored as

No decimal point is stored but the computer will ensure when data is moved in it is correctly aligned on the decimal point position. Similarly when the data is moved out or used for arithmetic, the decimal point is assumed to be between the second and third characters.

The V may appear anywhere in the picture string. If it is omitted then it is assumed to be after the last digit. Thus PIC 999V and PIC 999 have the same meaning.

The operational sign is represented by the picture character S which must be written at the beginning of the picture string. Thus a data item with PICTURE S99V9 can hold positive or negative numbers in the range -99.9 to +99.9. The way the sign is stored is the responsibility of the implementor and should not concern the programmer. (It is normally stored using a spare bit in the first or last character with the result that no extra storage is required for the S)

The picture characters V and S are intended for the storage of data items within the computer. We will look in the next chapter at some different characters which are used when we wish to output a decimal point or a sign.

7.2 THE USAGE CLAUSE

The USAGE clause is used in a data description entry to indicate the form in which the data is to be stored.

    USAGE IS DISPLAY

can be used with any data item to indicate that the data is to be stored in character format — that is each character of data is stored in a separate character of storage (6 bits on some computers and 8 bits on others).

Thus

    COUNT-ITEM PIC 999 USAGE IS DISPLAY.

occupies 3 characters of storage.

For numeric data we can instead write

    USAGE IS COMPUTATIONAL (or COMP for short).

This will ensure that the data is stored in the most efficient form for computation (ie arithmetic). The precise form chosen is the responsibility of the implementor. Common choices are packed decimal (each character stored in 4-bits) or pure binary. Thus if you write USAGE IS COMP with a numeric data item it will normally save storage space and speed up arithmetic. So COMP would be used for items which are used predominantly for arithmetic or are stored on magnetic media where economic use of storage is important. Original input (terminals, punched cards, etc) and output (to a terminal or printer) will invariably be USAGE IS DISPLAY.

The word IS is optional and USAGE can also be omitted so you can just write DISPLAY or COMP. If the whole clause is omitted then USAGE DISPLAY is assumed. So all the data items we have defined so far have been USAGE DISPLAY.

7.3 MOVING OF NUMERIC DATA ITEMS

Up to now we have avoided the question of what happens when numeric data is moved to a data item which is too large or too small for it. In all the examples so far the data being moved consisted of exactly the same number of characters as the receiving data item. This need not be the case and we will now see what happens in other cases.

The rules for numeric data are

— the data is aligned on the assumed decimal point

— digits on either end, that do not fit, are omitted (this is known as *truncation*)

— any spare digit positions in the receiving field are zero filled

Thus if 25.73 is moved to a data item AVERAGE with PICTURE 99V99 (eg MOVE 25.73 TO AVERAGE) the decimal points (actual or assumed) are aligned:

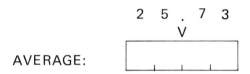

AVERAGE:

and then the data is moved in

```
            V
AVERAGE:  | 2   5   7   3 |
```

Note that in these diagrams V is used to show the position of the assumed decimal point.

If we moved 5.734 into the same field — the decimal points would again be aligned

```
      5 . 7 3 4
        V
  |             |
```

So even though the number has the same number of digits as the receiving data item they cannot all be accommodated. So the 4 is truncated and a zero is moved into the unused first character position:

```
         V
  | 0   5   7   3 |
```

(The computer could not store the number as

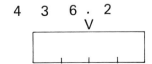

because this would be interpreted as 57.34.)

If we moved the number 436.2 into this field — the decimal points would again be aligned

```
  4   3   6 . 2
          V
  |             |
```

and this time the leading digit is truncated:

$$\overset{\text{V}}{\boxed{\begin{array}{c|c|c|c} 3 & 6 & 2 & 0 \end{array}}}$$

This might seem rather drastic, 436.2 suddenly becoming 36.2, but now that you are aware of the rule you must make sure that each data item is big enough for the largest value that will ever be moved into it. That is unless of course you have a requirement to remove the leading digits, in which case this is a convenient way to do it.

7.4 ARITHMETIC STATEMENTS

We have already seen how 1 can be added to a total by writing

    ADD 1 TO RECORD-COUNT

Instead of 1 we could write any numeric literal or in fact an identifier (of a numeric data item) eg

    ADD NEW-SALES TO TOTAL-SALES

The effect of this statement is to take the contents of NEW-SALES and add them to the contents of TOTAL-SALES.

For example

	before	after
NEW-SALES	25	25
TOTAL-SALES	50	75

It is also possible to specify a string of items to be added. For example the statement

    ADD NEW-SALES OLD-SALES TO TOTAL-SALES

has the effect

	before	after
NEW-SALES	25	25
OLD-SALES	10	10
TOTAL-SALES	50	85

It is also possible to add together some data items and store the result in a different data item overwriting its contents. This is done by using the GIVING version of ADD. For example

    ADD NEW-SALES TOTAL-SALES GIVING CURRENT-SALES

has the effect

	before	after
NEW-SALES	25	25
TOTAL-SALES	50	50
CURRENT-SALES	168	75

Note that the initial contents of CURRENT-SALES have no effect on the results of the addition.

The three other basic arithmetic verbs (SUBTRACT, MULTIPLY and DIVIDE) work in a similar way. Some examples are

(i)   SUBTRACT DEBITS CHARGES FROM BALANCE

This subtracts DEBITS and CHARGES from BALANCE:

	before	after
DEBITS	10	10
CHARGES	5	5
BALANCE	35	20

(ii)   SUBTRACT DEBITS CHARGES FROM BALANCE GIVING NEW-BALANCE.

This subtracts DEBITS and CHARGES from BALANCE and stores the result in NEW-BALANCE:

	before	after
DEBITS	10	10
CHARGES	5	5
BALANCE	35	35
NEW-BALANCE	65.4	20

(iii)   MULTIPLY PRICE BY TAX-RATE GIVING TAX-DUE

This statement multiplies PRICE and TAX-RATE and stores the result in TAX-DUE:

	before	after
PRICE	50	50
TAX-RATE	1.2	1.2
TAX-DUE	4000	60

(iv)   DIVIDE 12 INTO ANNUAL-SALES GIVING MONTHLY-SALES

The result of dividing ANNUAL-SALES by 12 is stored in MONTHLY-SALES:

	before	after
ANNUAL-SALES	120	120
MONTHLY-SALES	16.2	10

You will notice that the result field is always the last one named. The other data items are unchanged by execution of the statement. Any field, apart from the result field, may be an identifier or a numeric literal.

7.5 ARITHMETIC EXPRESSIONS AND COMPUTE

Coding complicated calculations using ADD, SUBTRACT, MULTIPLY and DIVIDE can be rather tedious. For such situations we have the COMPUTE verb. For example if we want to calculate TOTAL-PAY:

```
MULTIPLY BASIC BY BASIC-RATE GIVING BASIC-PAY

MULTIPLY OVERTIME BY OVERTIME-RATE GIVING OVERTIME-PAY

ADD BASIC-PAY OVERTIME-PAY GIVING TOTAL-PAY
```

can be replaced by the single statement

```
COMPUTE TOTAL-PAY = BASIC * BASIC-RATE

                  + OVERTIME * OVERTIME-RATE
```

In this statement BASIC * BASIC-RATE indicates that BASIC and BASIC-RATE are to be multiplied together, likewise for OVERTIME * OVERTIME-RATE. The + indicates that the results of these two multiplications are to be added together. The final result is then stored in TOTAL-PAY.

Apart from * for multiplication and + for addition, we can also use − for subtraction, / for division and ** for exponentiation. The order of evaluation is given by the following *precedence rules* which are the same as in algebra:

1)   all exponentiation in the expression from left to right

2)   all multiplication and division from left to right

3)   all addition and subtraction from left to right.

This sequence can be overridden by brackets − the expressions in the innermost brackets are evaluated before evaluating anything outside them.

For example the order of evaluation in the following expression is indicated by the numbers below the symbols

```
A + B * C / (A − B / C) + D ** E ** F * G / H
9   5   6   2   1   10   3    4    7   8
```

The expression in the bracket is evaluated first starting with the / and then applying the −. This takes care of the bracketed expression so the precedence rules are then applied to the rest of the expression.

Thus rules exist for writing expressions of great complexity but in practice calculations are rarely any more complex than the COMPUTE TOTAL-PAY statement above.

Note that the symbols + − * / and ** are in fact reserved words. So do not forget to leave a space on either side of them.

The coding after = in the COMPUTE statement is an example of an *arithmetic expression*. Arithmetic expressions may also appear on either side of the relational operator (=, <, >, etc) in a relational condition. Thus we can write

```
IF BASIC-PAY + OVERTIME-PAY > 200

   PERFORM LIMIT-CHECK

END-IF
```

and

```
PERFORM READ-BATCH
    UNTIL RECORD-COUNT = BATCH-COUNT - 3
```

7.6 SUMMARY

In this chapter we have looked at

Picture clauses for numeric data

— characters 9, V and S

The USAGE clause

— DISPLAY and COMPUTATION

Rules for moving numeric data

— alignment on the decimal point

— truncation

— zero filling

The Arithmetic Statements

— ADD

— SUBTRACT

— MULTIPLY

— DIVIDE

— COMPUTE

Arithmetic Expressions

QUIZ

1. What pictures are appropriate for data items which store values in the range

    (a)   0 to 49.75
    (b)   0 to .999
    (c)   80 to 160
    (d)   −3 to 18
    (e)   −.01 to 450

2. In PICTURE 9999 where is the assumed decimal point?

3. Show how data would be stored in CURRENT-RATE after executing MOVE NEW-RATE TO CURRENT-RATE in each of the following cases

| | NEW-RATE | | CURRENT-RATE |
	PICTURE	CONTENTS	PICTURE
(a)	V99	2,5	99V99
(b)	V99	2,5	99
(c)	999	2,5,1	9V9
(d)	9V9	5,6	99V99

4. Assume that before execution of each of these statements, A, B, C, D and E have values 2, 4, 8, 20 and −1 respectively, and they all have PICTURE S99. What are the values of each identifier after executing each of the following:

    (a) ADD A B TO C
    (b) ADD A E TO C
    (c) ADD A TO B GIVING C
    (d) SUBTRACT B FROM D
    (e) SUBTRACT B FROM D GIVING E
    (f) MULTIPLY B BY C GIVING D
    (g) MULTIPLY B BY C
    (h) DIVIDE A INTO D
    (i) DIVIDE D BY A
    (j) DIVIDE D BY A GIVING C
    (k) DIVIDE D BY C GIVING B REMAINDER E

5. Write down a COMPUTE statement to find the average value of THIS-MONTH and LAST-MONTH and store the result in MONTH-AVERAGE.

OTHER FEATURES

1. The SIGN Clause

When we write PICTURE S999 we do not normally want to worry about where or how the sign is actually stored. There is a notable exception to this. When signed numeric data is being input we must ensure that the position of the sign in the input data is consistent with the data item which receives it. This can be achieved by writing, for example

    PIC S999 SIGN LEADING SEPARATE

to indicate that the sign is at the beginning of the data item and is stored as a separate character.

2. The SYNCHRONIZED Clause

Most computer memories are organised in such a way that there are natural addressing boundaries such as word boundaries. A word might for example contain 2, 4, 8 or 10 characters. If no special action is taken some data items will start on word boundaries and some will start part way through a word and perhaps end part way through another word. Since most computers can process whole words more efficiently than individual characters there is an overhead in extracting the characters from the words. Much of this overhead is avoided for data items which have the SYNCHRONIZED (SYNC for short) clause in their description. It causes the data item to be aligned on the machine's natural boundaries. This results in some character positions being wasted. So the data occupies more space but it can be handled more efficiently.

The precise implications of this clause depend on the compiler being used.

3. Multiple Result Fields

If we want to add the same value to different data items we can do it as follows

    ADD SALES TO REGION-SALES

    ADD SALES TO TOTAL-SALES

However, we could instead combine them into one statement:

    ADD SALES TO REGION-SALES TOTAL-SALES

A similar facility is available with the other arithmetic statements.

4.   The ROUNDED Option

With any of the arithmetic statements it is possible to "round" the results.

As we have seen, without the ROUNDED option, any digits which cannot be accommodated in the result are truncated. Consider the example

    DIVIDE SALES BY NO-OF-SALESMEN

        GIVING AVERAGE-SALES

where AVERAGE-SALES has PICTURE 99V99. The following table shows some actual results of the division. For each actual result the truncated result (given by the above statement) and the rounded result are shown

actual result	truncated result	rounded result
30.011	30.01	30.01
30.014	30.01	30.01
30.015	30.01	30.02
30.019	30.01	30.02

To obtain the rounded result we simply write ROUNDED after the data item which receives the result. So for the above example we write

    DIVIDE SALES BY NO-OF-SALESMEN

        GIVING AVERAGE-SALES ROUNDED

5.   The SIZE ERROR Option

Earlier in this chapter we saw how leading digits in the result of an arithmetic operation can be truncated without warning. However, you can check if the result is too large for the data item which is to receive it by using the ON SIZE ERROR phrase. For example you can write

    MULTIPLY QUANTITY BY UNIT-PRICE

        GIVING TOTAL-PRICE

        ON SIZE ERROR PERFORM PRICE-OVERFLOW

    END-MULTIPLY

If the result of the calculation is too large for TOTAL-PRICE the statement PERFORM PRICE-OVERFLOW is executed.

The SIZE ERROR clause can be used with all the arithmetic statements.

6.   The CORRESPONDING Option

The CORRESPONDING option may be used with ADD and SUBTRACT in the same way as it is used with MOVE. You are however unlikely to find many instances where this is useful.

8   Report Production

Figure 8.1 shows two pages from a typical printed report. It contains sales figures for the sales-men in a company's Eastern Region and Western Region. To produce reports such as this we need to know about:

1. *Page handling*: how to move on to a new page for a different region, how to print a heading at the top of the page and a footing at the bottom.

2. *Line handling*: how to leave blank lines when they are needed to improve the appearance of the report.

3. *Data item handling*: how to present data in the form we are used to seeing it — without lead-ing zeros, with currency signs or minus signs next to the first digit, etc.

We will start with page handling.

MONTHLY SALES — EASTERN REGION MARCH 1981

SALESMAN	SALES	TARGET
BROWN, P. R.	£11,014.43	£10,000.00
COWEN, M.	£7,643.21	£10,000.00
EAGLE, S. R. V.	£5,361.12	£8,000.00
MARPLE, C. C.	£18,635.21	£15,000.00
NORTON, P. T.	£12,436.11	£10,000.00
PEOVER, Z.	£15,444.36	£15,000.00
TAYLOR, B. S.	£4,395.88	£15,000.00
THOMPSON, H.	£16,204.79	£15,000.00

TOTAL STAFF 8   TOTAL SALES £91,135.11

PAGE 4

MONTHLY SALES — WESTERN REGION MARCH 1981

SALESMAN	SALES	TARGET
DOOGLE, B.	£14,613.12	£10,000.00
HASTINGS, S.	£9,413.21	£10,000.00
JENKINS, P.	£7,613.28	£8,000.00
KENYON, S. L.	£18,694.77	£15,000.00
UMPLEBY, F.	£13,413.61	£12,000.00

TOTAL STAFF 5   TOTAL SALES £63,747.99

PAGE 5

Figure 8.1 Extract From Typical Report

8.1 WRITE AFTER ADVANCING

Each page in our sample report has two lines in fixed positions at the top of the page (the page heading and the column heading) and one line in a fixed position at the bottom of each page (we call this the *footing* line). In between there are a number of other lines: the ordinary lines each containing the details for one salesman (the *detail* lines) and the line containing summary information (the *total* line). A convenient way to define these lines is as shown in figure 8.2. Each type of line is defined as a separate record in the Working Storage Section and the print file record is used purely to store each line immediately prior to printing.

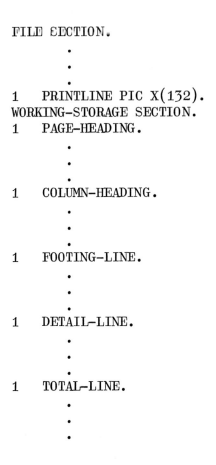

Figure 8.2 The Print Records

We have already seen that we can print the heading as follows

MOVE PAGE-HEADING TO PRINTLINE

WRITE PRINTLINE

or the equivalent coding

WRITE PRINTLINE FROM PAGE-HEADING

This, however, will print the page heading on the next available line. If we wish to print anywhere else we must use the ADVANCING option of the WRITE statement. The format we need here is

WRITE record-name FROM identifier-1

[AFTER ADVANCING $\left\{\begin{Bmatrix} \text{identifier-2} \\ \text{integer} \\ \underline{\text{PAGE}} \end{Bmatrix} \begin{Bmatrix} \text{LINE} \\ \text{LINES} \end{Bmatrix}\right\}$]

To print the page heading at the top of the next page we simply use

```
WRITE PRINTLINE FROM PAGE-HEADING
    AFTER ADVANCING PAGE
```

For the column heading line we wish to advance two lines and then print so we need

```
WRITE PRINTLINE FROM COLUMN-HEADING
    AFTER ADVANCING 2 LINES
```

where you will note that the words ADVANCING and LINES are optional.

For the detail lines we only advance one line before printing so we use

```
WRITE PRINTLINE FROM DETAIL-LINE
    AFTER ADVANCING 1 LINE
```

In Standard COBOL we can obtain the same effect with

```
WRITE PRINTLINE FROM DETAIL-LINE
```

but this statement does not make it so clear to the human reader of the program that the records are being printed.

To print the total line we need

```
WRITE PRINTLINE FROM TOTAL-LINE
    AFTER ADVANCING 2 LINES
```

Printing the footing line (the page number) is however more tricky because it is not a fixed number of lines from the previous line (the total line): the distance depends on how many salesmen there are in the region. The footing line is however a fixed position on the page so if we know where the total line is printed we can calculate how many lines must be advanced with a calculation such as

```
SUBTRACT CURRENT-LINE FROM FOOTING-POSITION GIVING SLEW
```

We can then cause the stationery to advance the number of lines stored in SLEW with

```
WRITE PRINTLINE FROM FOOTING-LINE
    AFTER ADVANCING SLEW LINES
```

8.2 THE LINAGE CLAUSE

In our example we have so far ignored the problem which would be caused if we could not fit all the salesmen for one region on one page. In general we must allow for such an overflow and, when it happens, print the footing line and then reprint the page heading and column heading at the top of the next page. It is also normal practice to allow a few blank lines at the top and bottom of each page.

This can all be done by keeping a check on the current position on the page and executing the page end processing when a pre-specified position is reached. This is possible using the COBOL we have already covered. It can, however, be automated by using the LINAGE clause. An example of the LINAGE clause is shown in figure 8.3.

```
FD REPORT-FILE
    LABEL RECORDS OMITTED
    LINAGE 60 LINES
        FOOTING AT 57
        LINES AT TOP 4
        LINES AT BOTTOM 2.
```

Figure 8.3   The LINAGE Clause

This linage clause specifies the page layout shown in figure 8.4. Printing can only take place within the page body. When an attempt is made to write beyond the page body the printer

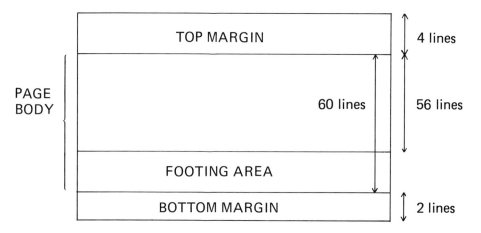

Figure 8.4   Page Layout

advances over the bottom margin and top margin of the next page. The footing area (which in our case starts at line 57 of the page body) provides an early warning system. Attempts to write in the footing area can be trapped by using the END-OF-PAGE option of WRITE. We can for example code

```
WRITE PRINTLINE FROM DETAIL-LINE
    AFTER ADVANCING 1 LINE
    AT END-OF-PAGE PERFORM PAGE-CHANGE
END-WRITE
```

When the footing area is reached this WRITE statement will print DETAIL-LINE as normal and then the statement following END-OF-PAGE is executed. So in this case PAGE-CHANGE is performed. This gives us the opportunity to print any page footings and page headings before proceeding to print the next detail line.

8.3   PICTURE EDITING

We have now seen how we can produce well laid out reports by spacing the lines and proceeding to a new page when appropriate. An equally important aspect of report production is the presentation of individual data items in a form which is easily understood. For example if we printed the data item

03 BALANCE PIC 9(5)V99

when it had the value 123.45 the following would be printed:

0012345

It is however essential that the decimal point is printed:

00123.45

It is also desirable for the leading zeros to be removed

123.45

Sometimes we will want to print negative values:

−123.45

or a value preceded by a currency sign

£123.45

All these can be achieved by moving ordinary numeric data items (defined using picture characters "9", "S" and "V") into *numeric edited* data items — these are data items with picture character 9 and other special characters such as "." and "-" and "£".

8.4 DECIMAL POINT INSERTION

An actual decimal point can be inserted in a data item by writing a decimal point at the desired point in the picture.

Take, for example the following coding

3 STORED-VALUE   PIC 99V999

3 PRINT-VALUE   PIC 999.99

⋅
⋅
⋅

MOVE STORED-VALUE TO PRINT-VALUE

The following shows some examples of the effect of this MOVE statement:

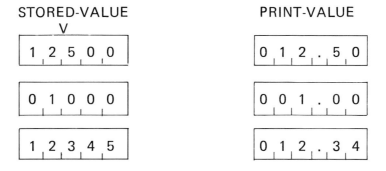

The assumed decimal point of the data being moved is aligned with the actual decimal point. The characters are then moved in. Truncation and zero filling rules apply as for ordinary numeric data items. The same rules of alignment, truncation and zero filling apply to all numeric edited items.

Unlike the V, the decimal point occupies a character of storage. It may not be the last character in a picture and it cannot appear in the same picture as a V.

8.5 ZERO SUPPRESSION

Leading zeros in a data item may be suppressed by use of the picture character Z. Each Z in a picture character indicates that that position contains a digit unless the digit moved in is a leading zero, whereupon it is replaced by a space.

Take the example

```
3 STORED-COUNT  PIC 9(5).
3 PRINT-COUNT    PIC ZZZ99.
        .
        .
        .
    MOVE STORED-COUNT TO PRINT-COUNT
```

The following shows some examples of the effect of this MOVE

STORED-COUNT	PRINT-COUNT
0 0 0 0 1	0 1
0 0 0 1 2	1 2
0 0 1 2 3	1 2 3
0 1 0 0 3	1 0 0 3

Note in the first example only the first three leading zeros are suppressed because they are the only ones which corresponded with a Z in PRINT-COUNT's picture. Note also in the last example that only the leading zero is removed — not the one in the third position.

Normally you will want to suppress leading zeros in all positions except the units position. So a more likely picture for PRINT-COUNT is ZZZZ9.

8.6 SIGN INSERTION

Just as we needed a printable form of V so also do we need a printable form of S. In fact there are four different sign characters but here we will confine ourselves to the one most commonly used — the minus sign.

An example of its use is shown in the following coding

```
03  PRINT-VALUE PIC -999
```

   The character position corresponding to "—" will contain a minus sign if the number moved in is negative and will contain space otherwise. For example:

MOVE statement	PRINT-VALUE
MOVE 1 to PRINT-VALUE	0 0 1
MOVE 123 to PRINT-VALUE	1 2 3
MOVE -1 TO PRINT-VALUE	— 0 0 1
MOVE -123 TO PRINT-VALUE	— 1 2 3

   This picture is unsatisfactory because we have not suppressed the leading zero. We could write PIC–ZZ9 but this would then cause a gap between the sign and the number when we suppressed the leading zeros.

   What we really want is for the leading zeros to be suppressed and the minus sign to move next to the most significant digit.

   This is achieved with the following example

03   PRINT-VALUE PIC ———9

Let us see some examples

MOVE statement	PRINT-VALUE
MOVE 1 TO PRINT-VALUE	1
MOVE 123 TO PRINT-VALUE	1 2 3
MOVE -1 TO PRINT-VALUE	— 1
MOVE -123 TO PRINT-VALUE	— 1 2 3

   Thus the leading zeros are removed. The sign (whether it be the minus sign or blank) is then stored immediately before the first digit.

   In these examples literals have been the subject of the MOVE. The same rules would however apply if a data item described with picture character picture S had been moved.

8.7 THE CURRENCY SIGN

A currency sign may be inserted at the beginning of a data item. We can for example write

   03 BALANCE PIC £££9

if the pound sign is the currency sign we are using. Written like this it works like the floating minus sign except that a pound sign appears before the most significant digit rather than a minus sign or a space. For example

MOVE statement	BALANCE
MOVE 1 TO BALANCE	£ 1
MOVE 500 BALANCE	£ 5 0 0

Your compiler will have as its currency sign either the currency sign of the country the compiler is being used in or the currency sign of the country of origin of the compiler.

If it is not the sign you want you can alter it to any other character that the computer recognises provided it is not used for any other purpose in the picture clause. This is done in the SPECIAL-NAMES paragraph that follows the OBJECT-COMPUTER in the Environment Division. If you want to use F for Franc, for example, you declare it:

SPECIAL-NAMES.

    CURRENCY SIGN IS "F".

8.8 SIMPLE INSERTION CHARACTERS

There are four characters which can be inserted at any point in a data item

Picture character	Character inserted
,	,
/	/
B	space
0	0 (zero)

They are simply inserted in the data item in the position indicated by their position in the picture. For example with

03 STORED-DATE   PIC 9(6).
03 PRINT-DATE   PIC 99/99/99.
      .
      .
      .

    MOVE STORED-DATE TO PRINT-DATE

the character '/' will be inserted between the second and third and between the fourth and fifth characters of STORED-DATE. For example

STORED-DATE	PRINT-DATE (after above MOVE)
1 0 1 1 8 0	1 0 / 1 1 / 8 0

8.9 OTHER ASPECTS OF EDITING

For simplicity each editing character has been presented independently but you can use sensible combinations of them such as

---9.9

£££9.9

Z,ZZ9.9

ZZZ900

The full rules for the use of all these characters and a few more are given in the *Reference Summary.*

Besides the numeric edited data items described we also have *alphanumeric edited* data items. These consist of the character X and the simple insertion characters 'O', 'B' and '/'.

Unlike S and V all the editing characters actually occupy storage space – one character of storage for each character in the picture string.

Edited fields *cannot* be described as USAGE COMPUTATIONAL – not even ones like 99900 which are purely numeric.

8.10 THE ACCEPT STATEMENT

On printed reports it is common for the date to appear in the page heading. The current-date can be obtained in a data item RUN-DATE, for example, by using the following COBOL code

```
3 RUN-DATE  PIC 9(6).
```

```
  ACCEPT RUN-DATE FROM DATE
```

The date is obtained in the format YYMMDD where YY is the year, MM is the month and DD is the day. Thus on 13th January 1981 the above statement would store 810113 in RUN-DATE.

It is also possible to get the time of the day by writing

```
ACCEPT identifier FROM TIME.
```

8.11 SUMMARY

In this chapter we have covered

- the ADVANCING Option of WRITE for advancing the printer a given number of lines or to a new page

- the LINAGE clause which automates some of the page end processing

- Picture Editing characters '.' 'Z' '-' '£' ',' '/' 'B' and '0'

- Numeric Edited and Alphanumeric Edited data items

- ACCEPT DATE and TIME.

QUIZ

1. The printer is on line 6 of the page when the following coding is executed

    ```
    WRITE PRINTLINE FROM HEADING-2 AFTER 3
    WRITE PRINTLINE FROM HEADING-3 AFTER 2
    ```

    (a) Which line is HEADING-2 printed on?

    (b) How many blank lines are there between HEADING-2 and HEADING-3?

    (c) Which line does the printer end up on?

2. Study the following linage clause

    ```
    LINAGE 32
        FOOTING AT 25
        LINES AT TOP 5
        LINES AT BOTTOM 3
    ```

    (a) How many lines are there in the whole page?

    (b) Which is the first line you can print on?

    (c) Which is the first line on which printing causes the end of page clause to be executed?

3. What is the result when data is moved into the data items as shown below?

	Data	Picture of receiving data item
(a)	43.61	999.99
(b)	43.61	99.9
(c)	43.61	99.
(d)	0	ZZ99
(e)	1004	ZZZ9
(f)	16	−999
(g)	16	−−−9
(h)	−16	−−−9
(i)	16	£999
(j)	4318	9,999
(k)	0	9,999
(l)	0	Z,ZZ9
(m)	−5.2	S99.99

    Note: for the last two check the *Reference Summary*.

4. Write coding to store the hour of the day in a data item called HOUR-OF-DAY (hint: refer to format-2 of the ACCEPT statement).

OTHER FEATURES

1.   LINAGE Clause and LINAGE-COUNTER

Instead of specifying integers in the LINAGE clause, data-names may be specified. As a result the size of the page, footing area, top margin and bottom margin may each change during the execution of the program.

Whenever the LINAGE clause is used the compiler generates a special register called LINAGE-COUNTER. A *special register* is a data item automatically generated by the compiler. It can be referenced like other data items but it is not defined by the programmer. LINAGE-COUNTER contains 1 when the printer is positioned at the start of the page body. It is automatically updated, every time a line is written, to contain the current position within the page body.

2.   Extra Picture Characters

There are a few other Picture characters which are used less frequently.

+   this can be used instead of the minus sign in the PICTURE clause. It works exactly like the minus sign except that if the number is positive a plus sign is inserted in the appropriate position instead of a space. Incidentally, both the plus sign and the minus sign may appear at the end of the picture string instead of the beginning.

CR   the two characters CR may appear at the end of a picture string. It works just like the minus sign. If the number moved in is negative, CR is inserted, otherwise two spaces are inserted.

DB   the two characters DB work in the same way as CR, being inserted if a negative number is moved in and spaces being inserted otherwise. The choice between CR (short for credit) and DB (short for debit) would depend on whether credits or debits were represented as negative numbers in the program being written.

P   this is a padding character used when the assumed decimal point is outside the scope of the data item. For example if numbers in the range .001 to .099 are to be stored we would only need a two character data item with the decimal point one position to the left of it:

Thus .013 would be stored | 1 | 3 |

To indicate that the decimal point is one place to the left we write

        PICTURE VP99

If for example the decimal point had been three positions to the right of the data item we would write

        PICTURE 99PPPV

*   The character * may be used in place of Z as a zero suppression character. When this is used leading zeros are replaced by asterisks instead of spaces.

3.   BLANK WHEN ZERO Clause

BLANK WHEN ZERO may be written in the data description entry of numeric or numeric edited data items. Its effect is to fill the data item with spaces whenever the value zero is moved into it.

4.   DECIMAL POINT IS COMMA Clause

This clause is designed for use in those countries where the roles of the decimal point and comma are interchanged. If DECIMAL POINT IS COMMA is written in the SPECIAL-NAMES paragraph then the functions of the decimal point and comma are exchanged in the PICTURE clause and numeric literals throughout the program. Thus comma is used as an actual decimal point in pict ure strings and literals and the dot becomes a simple insertion character.

9 Table Handling

We are all accustomed to using tables in everyday life — tables showing votes cast for political candidates:

Candidate	Votes cast
BUTLER	12,643
SMITH	4,653
THOMLINSON	24,911
WAITE	412

football league tables, timetables and so on.

In the business world we have, for example, tables showing a company's sales split down by area:

AREA	AREA-TOTAL
1	6541.28
2	4932.63
3	4400.95
4	9400.43
5	3941.50

This chapter is concerned with processing tables such as this in COBOL.

Let's assume that we have a sales file in which each record, corresponding to one sale, contains, amongst other details, an area-code (1, 2, 3, 4 or 5) and a sales-value (see figure 9.1). We will start by seeing how the above sales table can be produced from this file.

97

```
FD  SALES-FILE  ....
1   SALES-RECORD.
    3  AREA-CODE          PIC 9.
    3  MONTH-NUMBER       PIC 9.
    3  SALES-VALUE        PIC 9(5)V99.
    3  SALES-QUANTITY     PIC 9(4).
```

Figure 9.1 The Sales File

9.1 DEFINING AND USING TABLES

We could define the table as follows

```
1   AREA-TOTAL-TABLE.
    3  AREA-TOTAL-1   PIC 9(7)V99.
    3  AREA-TOTAL-2   PIC 9(7)V99.
    3  AREA-TOTAL-3   PIC 9(7)V99.
    3  AREA-TOTAL-4   PIC 9(7)V99.
    3  AREA-TOTAL-5   PIC 9(7)V99.
```

Then for each record read we would have to execute something like the following:

```
ADD-TO-TOTAL.
    EVALUATE AREA-CODE
    WHEN 1  ADD SALES-VALUE TO AREA-TOTAL-1
    WHEN 2  ADD SALES-VALUE TO AREA-TOTAL-2
    WHEN 3  ADD SALES-VALUE TO AREA-TOTAL-3
    WHEN 4  ADD SALES-VALUE TO AREA-TOTAL-4
    WHEN 5  ADD SALES-VALUE TO AREA-TOTAL-5
    END-EVALUATE
```

The definition and the procedural code are both extremely cumbersome and imagine what it would be like if there were 100 areas or a 1000!

What we really want to do when we define the table is say that

AREA-TOTAL occurs five times

and in the ADD-TO-TOTAL paragraph we want to say

ADD SALES-VALUE TO the AREA-TOTAL for AREA-CODE

This in fact is more or less what we write in COBOL (see figure 9.2).

```
WORKING-STORAGE SECTION.

1   AREA-TOTAL-TABLE.

  3  AREA-TOTAL         PIC 9(7)V99 OCCURS 5 TIMES.
        .
        .
        .

ADD-TO-TOTAL.
     ADD SALES-VALUE TO AREA-TOTAL (AREA-CODE)
```

Figure 9.2   Table Definition and Access

Since there is more than one AREA-TOTAL, whenever we refer to it we must indicate which one we mean. We do this by writing a *subscript* in brackets after AREA-TOTAL. The subscript may either be an integer or a data-name (qualified if desired) which represents a data item containing an integer. The integer in either case indicates which AREA-TOTAL you want to reference: 1 indicates the first one, 2 the second, and so on. It would thus be incorrect to use 0 or an integer which is negative or greater than 5 (in this example).

So some valid references to the table items are

```
ADD SALES-VALUE TO AREA-TOTAL (AREA-CODE)

ADD SALES-VALUE TO AREA-TOTAL (AREA-CODE OF SALES-RECORD)

ADD SALES-VALUE TO AREA-TOTAL (1)

ADD SALES-VALUE TO AREA-TOTAL (4)

ADD SALES-VALUE TO AREA-TOTAL (5)
```

We are *not*, however, allowed to write

```
ADD SALES-VALUE TO AREA-TOTAL

ADD SALES-VALUE TO AREA-TOTAL (0)

ADD SALES-VALUE TO AREA-TOTAL (-2)

ADD SALES-VALUE TO AREA-TOTAL (6)

ADD SALES-VALUE TO AREA-TOTAL (AREA-CODE + 3)

ADD SALES-VALUE TO AREA-TOTAL (CODE-NUMBER (4))
```

Note the last two examples. The subscript may not be an arithmetic expression or a subscripted data-name.

We would have to rewrite these two as

```
ADD AREA-CODE 3 GIVING AREA-SUBSCRIPT

ADD SALES-VALUE TO AREA-TOTAL (AREA-SUBSCRIPT)
```

and

```
MOVE CODE-NUMBER (4) TO AREA-SUBSCRIPT

ADD SALES-VALUE TO AREA-TOTAL (AREA-SUBSCRIPT)
```

where AREA-SUBSCRIPT would be a specially defined Working-Storage item with PICTURE 9.

Certain restrictions apply to the OCCURS clause. The main ones are

— the OCCURS clause may only be used with level numbers 2 to 49 (not 1 or 88)

— the OCCURS clause and a VALUE clause may not be used in the same data description entry

— a VALUE clause (except with level 88s) may not be used to describe a data item which is subordinate to an OCCURS clause.

9.2 TABLES OF GROUP ITEMS

The table we have defined is the most simple you could imagine. So let's now consider the following table:

AREA		AREA TOTALS
1	value	6541.28
	quantity	54
2	value	4932.63
	quantity	28
3	value	4400.95
	quantity	26
4	value	9400.43
	quantity	64
5	value	3941.50
	quantity	22

We still have an entry in the table for each area but this time the entry is made up of two items — the sales value total and the sales quantity total.

Thus when we come to represent this table in COBOL we still have AREA-TOTAL (or more appropriately now AREA-TOTALS) occurring five times but this time it is subdivided into VALUE-TOTAL and QUANTITY-TOTAL (see figure 9.3).

You will notice that since VALUE-TOTAL and QUANTITY-TOTAL are repeated items we must use a subscript whenever we refer to them. If we wished to refer to AREA-TOTALS we would also of course need a subscript.

eg MOVE AREA-TOTALS (1) TO AREA-TOTALS-STORE

In fact we use a subscript with any data item which has an OCCURS clause in its description or is subordinate to such a data item.

```
1    AREA-TOTAL-TABLE.
 3   AREA-TOTALS                        OCCURS 5 TIMES.
  5 VALUE-TOTAL        PIC 9(7)V99.
  5 QUANTITY-TOTAL  PIC 9(6).
          .
          .
          .
ADD-TO-TOTALS.
      ADD SALES-VALUE TO VALUE-TOTAL (AREA-CODE)
      ADD SALES-QUANTITY TO QUANTITY-TOTAL (AREA-CODE)
```

Figure 9.3   A Table of Group Items

9.3   TWO-DIMENSIONAL TABLES

Both tables we have looked at so far are *one-dimensional* — in other words we used one OCCURS clause to define them and used one subscript every time we accessed a table item.

Consider now the following table in which the sales have been split down into monthly figures for a three month period:

AREA		MONTH		
		1	2	3
1	value	2001.48	2435.25	2104.55
	quantity	16	20	18
2	value	1512.65	1987.25	1432.73
	quantity	8	12	8
3	value	1405.25	1789.23	1206.47
	quantity	8	11	7
4	value	2975.57	3456.50	2968.36
	quantity	20	24	20
5	value	1258.73	1513.59	1169.18
	quantity	7	9	6

This is an example of a *two-dimensional* table. Not only do we have sales totals for each area, but the whole set of area totals is repeated for each month.

The definition for each month (one column of the above table) is just like the definition we previously had for AREA-TOTAL-TABLE:

```
3    MONTHLY-TOTALS
 5   AREA-TOTALS                        OCCURS 5 TIMES.
  7 VALUE-TOTAL        PIC 9(7)V99.
  7 QUANTITY-TOTAL PIC 9(6).
```

All we need do to describe the full table is indicate that MONTHLY-TOTALS occurs 3 times:

```
1    SALES-TOTAL-TABLE.

  3    MONTHLY-TOTALS              OCCURS 3 TIMES.

    5    AREA-TOTALS              OCCURS 5 TIMES.

      7 VALUE-TOTAL    PIC 9(7)V99.

      7 QUANTITY-TOTAL PIC 9(6).
```

When we refer to MONTHLY-TOTALS we must indicate which month we are interested in Since it is a normal table item, this is done by means of a subscript:

```
MOVE MONTHLY-TOTALS (MONTH-NUMBER) TO MONTHLY-TOTALS-STORE.
```

When we refer to AREA-TOTALS, VALUE-TOTAL or QUANTITY-TOTAL not only do we have to indicate which month we are interested in but we also have to indicate the area. This is done by specifying two subscripts:

```
ADD SALES-VALUE TO VALUE-TOTAL (MONTH-NUMBER AREA-CODE)
```

The first subscript corresponds to the first OCCURS and the second subscript corresponds to the second OCCURS in the table definition.

When an item is subject to one OCCURS it needs one subscript; when it is subject to two it needs two subscripts. We can in fact go one further and have three OCCURS clauses nested inside each other. So we sometimes need three subscripts to uniquely identify a data item.

9.4   UNIQUENESS OF REFERENCE

Up till now the term *identifier* has been used to represent a data-name with or without qualifications. So (referring to the record definition in figure 9.1)

```
SALES-RECORD

MONTH-NUMBER

MONTH-NUMBER IN SALES-RECORD
```

are all valid identifiers.

Now we can extend the definition of identifier to include subscripted data-names and subscripted qualified data-names. So (referring to the above table definition)

```
MONTHLY-TOTALS (1)

QUANTITY-TOTAL (MONTH-NUMBER, 2)

VALUE-TOTAL OF SALES-TOTAL-TABLE (3 4)
```

are all valid identifiers.

Note that

—   you may, if you wish, have a comma immediately after the first subscript in a list (and after the second subscript in a list of three)

   —   you can mix integer and data-name subscripts

   —   if an identifier contains qualification and subscripts the qualification comes first (the subscripts refer to the entire qualified data-name, not just to the last qualifier)

The format for an identifier now becomes

$$\text{data-name-1}\left[\begin{Bmatrix}\underline{OF}\\\underline{IN}\end{Bmatrix}\text{data-name-2}\right]...\left[\begin{Bmatrix}\underline{OF}\\\underline{IN}\end{Bmatrix}\text{file-name}\right]$$

$$[(\text{subscript-1}\ [\text{subscript-2}\ [\text{subscript-3}]\,]\,)]$$

where subscript is either a positive integer or a (possibly qualified) data-name which references an elementary integer data item. The above format applies whenever "identifier" appears in a COBOL format.

Condition-names may also be qualified and subscripted in accordance with the same rules as data-names:

$$\text{condition-name}\left[\begin{Bmatrix}\underline{OF}\\\underline{IN}\end{Bmatrix}\text{data-name}\right]...\left[\begin{Bmatrix}\underline{OF}\\\underline{IN}\end{Bmatrix}\text{file-name}\right]$$

$$[(\text{subscript-1}\ [\text{subscript-2}\ [\text{subscript-3}]\,]\,)]$$

9.5 ASSIGNING INITIAL VALUES TO TABLES

Let's assume that we wish to define a table which contains the number of days in each month of the year. We will define it as follows

```
1   MONTH-TABLE.

3 DAYS-IN-MONTH PIC 99 OCCURS 12 TIMES.
```

This will define a data item with the following structure:

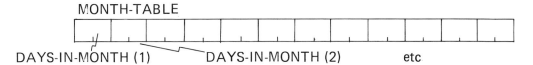

Thus we have 12 data items each of 2 characters length making a string of 24 characters. If we want to give the table an initial value we have the choice of giving it 12 two character values or one 24 character value — the two are equivalent when the data is stored as characters (ie USAGE DISPLAY).

The one 24 character value is easier:

```
1   MONTH-TABLE     VALUE "312831303130313130313031".

3 DAYS-IN-MONTH PIC 99 OCCURS 12 TIMES.
```

Note that a non-numeric literal must be used because the VALUE clause is at the group level.

Giving 12 two character values is in some ways more readable but it involves a lot more writing (see figure 9.4).

```
1   MONTH-VALUES.
    3  FILLER          PIC 99 VALUE 31.
    3  FILLER          PIC 99 VALUE 28.
    3  FILLER          PIC 99 VALUE 31.
    3  FILLER          PIC 99 VALUE 30.
    3  FILLER          PIC 99 VALUE 31.
    3  FILLER          PIC 99 VALUE 30.
    3  FILLER          PIC 99 VALUE 31.
    3  FILLER          PIC 99 VALUE 31.
    3  FILLER          PIC 99 VALUE 30.
    3  FILLER          PIC 99 VALUE 31.
    3  FILLER          PIC 99 VALUE 30.
    3  FILLER          PIC 99 VALUE 31.
1   MONTH-TABLE REDEFINES MONTH-VALUES.
    3  DAYS-IN-MONTH PIC 99 OCCURS 12 TIMES.
```

Figure 9.4   Using REDEFINES to Assign Values to a Table

You will notice that we have had to define a separate record with 12 two character data items (the same structure as the table) with each data item having the appropriate value. We must then tell the compiler that this record and the table are to occupy the same storage area. This is done by using the REDEFINES clause as shown in figure 9.4.

In general we can write

level-no data-name-1 <u>REDEFINES</u> data-name-2

to tell the compiler that the data items represented by data-name-1 and data-name-2 are to occupy the same storage locations. It is very much like the automatic redefinition at level 1 in the file section. The following rules apply to REDEFINES:

— the REDEFINES clause must be written immediately after the data-name (before any other clauses)

— data-name-1 and data-name-2 must have the same level number

— the entry containing the REDEFINES clause must immediately follow the definition of the area which is being redefined

— data-name-1 and data-name-2 must represent data items of equal length

— there must be no VALUE clause (except with level 88s) in the description of data-name-1 or any data item subordinate to it

— the REDEFINES clause may not be used at level 1 in the file section.

Returning to the question of assigning initial values to tables, we see that we have two methods: specifying the VALUE at the group level or using REDEFINES. The first method depends on the fact that the table items are stored in character form. Some situations in which you might have to use the second method are

— the table items are defined as COMPUTATIONAL

— the table items contain the PICTURE character S

— the table is more than 120 characters long (the maximum length of a non-numeric literal)

9.6 PERFORM WITH THE VARYING OPTION

Let's assume that we want to add up all the items in a table. Figure 9.5 shows some coding which will add each item in turn to a grand total

```
WORKING-STORAGE SECTION.
1   AREA-TOTAL-TABLE.
 3  AREA-TOTAL        PIC 9(7)V99 OCCURS 10 TIMES.
1   AREA-NUMBER       PIC 99.
1   GRAND-TOTAL       PIC 9(8)V99.

PROCEDURE DIVISION.
          .
          .
          .

    MOVE ZERO TO GRAND-TOTAL
    PERFORM ADD-TO-GRAND-TOTAL
       VARYING AREA-NUMBER FROM 1 BY 1
          UNTIL AREA-NUMBER > 10
          .
          .
          .

ADD-TO-GRAND-TOTAL.
    ADD AREA-TOTAL (AREA-NUMBER) TO GRAND-TOTAL.
```

Figure 9.5   Use of PERFORM with VARYING

You will note that we have used a new variation of PERFORM. Its effect is to execute the named paragraph, ADD-TO-GRAND-TOTAL, repeatedly until the condition AREA-NUMBER >10 is true. Each time it is executed the identifier following VARYING (AREA-NUMBER in this case) has a different value. For the first execution it takes the value specified after FROM (1 in this case). For each subsequent execution the value specified after BY (1 in this case) is added to the current value of the variable. So in this case ADD-TO-GRAND-TOTAL is performed with AREA-NUMBER equal to 1, then with it equal to 2, then 3 and so on all the way up to 10. When one more is added to AREA-NUMBER it becomes 11, so the condition AREA-NUMBER >10 becomes true and ADD-TO-GRAND-TOTAL is performed no more. Note that the named paragraph is *not* executed with AREA-NUMBER equal to 11.

The equivalent low level coding to this PERFORM ... VARYING statement is

```
MOVE 1 TO AREA-NUMBER
PERFORM UNTIL AREA-NUMBER > 10
    PERFORM ADD-TO-GRAND-TOTAL
    ADD 1 TO AREA-NUMBER
END-PERFORM
```

In general the initial value (specified after FROM) may be any numeric literal or numeric data item, as may be the increment (specified after BY). Any COBOL condition may be specified after UNTIL. The VARYING phrase may also be used with the in-line PERFORM statement.

9.7 SUMMARY

In this chapter we have covered

the OCCURS clause

—   for defining 1-dimensional tables

—   for defining 2- and 3-dimensional tables

—   for defining tables of group items

subscripts

a fuller definition of identifier

the REDEFINES clause

the VARYING option of PERFORM

QUIZ

1.   A file contains the result of a market survey of television viewing. The opinions of each person interviewed are stored in one record. The record contains the name of the person (30 characters) and the ten most popular television programs. For each program the name of the program (20 characters) and a popularity rating out of 20 marks are stored. Give a suitable definition for this record.

2.   Study the following coding and then answer the questions below

```
1     PRICE-LIST.
 3     BRAND                OCCURS 25.
  5     BRAND-SIZE          OCCURS 4.
   7 PRICE     PIC 999.
   7 DISCOUNT  PIC 99.
```

(a)   How many characters of storage does this table occupy?

(b)   How would the price of the second brand size of the fifteenth brand be referenced?

(c)   If the first character of PRICE-LIST is in position 1 what character positions do the following occupy

```
PRICE (1, 4)
DISCOUNT (1, 4)
BRAND-SIZE (2, 1)
BRAND (20)
```

3.   Given the definition in question 2 which of the following are valid identifiers?

   (a)   PRICE-LIST (1)

   (b)   BRAND-SIZE (DISCOUNT (2, 3))

   (c)   PRICE (4, 3) OF PRICE-LIST

   (d)   PRICE OF PRICE-LIST (4, 3)

   (e)   DISCOUNT (4, 15)

   (f)   PRICE OF BRAND-SIZE OF BRAND IN PRICE-LIST

   (g)   BRAND-SIZE (SIZE-CODE + 2)

4.   The following table items must all be assigned the value -1

```
1  MARKER-TABLE.
 3 MARKER   PIC S9 OCCURS 5.
```

   (a)   Use REDEFINES to assign the values

   (b)   Use PERFORM VARYING to assign the values

Indexes

In COBOL there is an alternative to subscripts for referencing table items, ie indexes. An *index* is defined as part of the OCCURS clause by writing

INDEXED BY index-name

The index-name can then be used instead of a subscript to uniquely identify a table item. The idea is that by associating the index with the table some compilers can make table access more efficient.

The index-name may be used as the FROM variable in a PERFORM statement and may be used in a COBOL condition. It may not be used in any of the other statements which process normal data items (in MOVE, ADD, etc). To alter the value of an index, or to transfer a value from one index to another we must use the special SET statement. If we wish to store the contents of an index we must use a special *index data item* defined using the clause USAGE IS INDEX.

Apart from any increase in efficiency the other benefit obtained from using indexes is that we can use the SEARCH statement on tables with indexes. There are two forms of SEARCH, both of which search a table looking for items which match a stated condition. The first form searches sequentially from any desired position. The second form which is potentially more efficient can only be used on tables which are stored in sequence. The sequence must be declared by using the ASCENDING/DESCENDING KEY option of the OCCURS clause.

10 Inter-program Communication

We have seen how what is popularly known as modular programming can be implemented by dividing a program up into sections, with the main control section PERFORMing other sections, which can in turn PERFORM further sections. By this means we can divide the Procedure Division into manageable units but it offers no help in dividing up the data. This problem can be solved by dividing large programs into a number of smaller programs. The main control program can then execute the other programs by using the CALL statement. Thus the modules consist of entire programs instead of sections within a program.

10.1 CALL AND EXIT PROGRAM

Let's assume that we are going to divide a validation program (see figure 10.1) into a main control program (VALIDATION-CONTROL) and separate programs for each validation routine (ACCOUNT-NO-CHECK, DATE-CHECK and READING-CHECK).

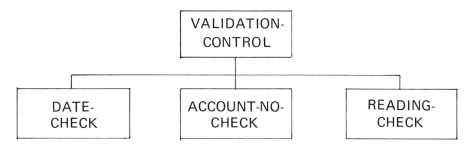

Figure 10.1 Structure of Validation Program

Each of these programs will consist of the normal four divisions. In addition to normal COBOL statements there will be statements for transferring control between the programs (see figure 10.2).

At the point in VALIDATION-CONTROL where the program DATE-CHECK is to be executed we write CALL "DATE-CHECK". This transfers control to the first statement in the Procedure Division of the *called program:* DATE-CHECK. This program is then executed normally until an EXIT PROGRAM statement is encountered. This statement causes control to return to the *calling program*, VALIDATION-CONTROL, and within that program execution continues with the statement after the CALL.

```
            IDENTIFICATION DIVISION.

            PROGRAM-ID.  VALIDATION-CONTROL.
                     .
                     .
                     .
            PROCEDURE DIVISION.
                     .
                     .
                     .
                CALL "DATE-CHECK" - - - -→- - -
                         .
                         .
                         .


            IDENTIFICATION DIVISION.

            PROGRAM-ID.  DATE-CHECK.
                     .
                     .
                     .
            PROCEDURE DIVISION.←- - - - - - - -
                     .
                     .
                     .
                EXIT PROGRAM. - -→- -
```

Figure 10.2   Transferring Control Between Programs

The EXIT PROGRAM must appear in a paragraph by itself. COBOL permits you to write any number of EXIT PROGRAMs in a program. However, structured programming advocates would recommend the use of just one — at the end of the main section of the program.

The called program, DATE-CHECK in this case, can CALL another program. The only restriction is that a program may not CALL itself either directly or indirectly (through a chain of CALLs).

The group of programs consisting of a main program and all the programs it calls directly and indirectly is known as a *run unit*.

10.2   DATA LINKAGE

We have now seen how to pass control between programs. For this to be of practical value we must also be able to pass data. For example, VALIDATION-CONTROL will need to pass a date to DATE-CHECK and DATE-CHECK will need to return a flag which indicates whether or not the date is valid.

The data items which are passed between programs are known as *parameters*.

Each parameter must

1.   appear in the USING phrase of CALL

2.   appear in the USING phrase of the Procedure Division header of the called program

3.   be defined in the Linkage Section of the called program.

An example appears in figure 10.3.

```
IDENTIFICATION DIVISION.
PROGRAM-ID.  VALIDATION-CONTROL.
        .
        .

WORKING-STORAGE SECTION.
1   DATE-STORE  PIC 9(6).
1   ERROR-FLAG  PIC 9.
 88 DATE-ERROR              VALUE 1.
        .
        .

PROCEDURE DIVISION.
        .
        .


    MOVE METER-DATE TO DATE-STORE
    CALL "DATE-CHECK" USING DATE-STORE ERROR-FLAG
    IF DATE-ERROR . . .
        .
        .


IDENTIFICATION DIVISION.
PROGRAM-ID. DATE-CHECK.
        .
        .

DATA DIVISION.
        .
        .

LINKAGE SECTION.
1   INPUT-DATE.
 3  IN-DAY      PIC 99.
 3  IN-MONTH    PIC 99.
 3  IN-YEAR     PIC 99.
1   ERROR-FLAG  PIC 9.
PROCEDURE DIVISION     USING INPUT-DATE ERROR-FLAG.

    .
    .

    MOVE 0 TO ERROR-FLAG

    .
    .

    MOVE 1 TO ERROR-FLAG

    .
    .

    EXIT PROGRAM.
```

Figure 10.3   Data Linkage Between Programs

In our example there are two parameters so two identifiers must appear in USING phrases of the CALL statement and the Procedure Division header of the called program. The parameters are matched by their positions in the lists. Thus the first parameter in CALL — DATE-STORE — corresponds with the first one in the Procedure Division header — INPUT-DATE. Similarly ERROR-FLAG in the CALL corresponds to ERROR-FLAG in the Procedure Division header. The names used for the parameters only have meaning within their own program so you are free to give corresponding parameters the same or different names, whichever is appropriate for the circumstances.

The parameters in the CALL statement must all be defined as level 1 data items in the calling program. The parameters in the Procedure Division header must all be defined as level 1 data items in the Linkage Section in the called program's Data Division. Records in the Linkage Section are defined in the same way as the Working Storage Section except the VALUE clause may not be used. The definition of each parameter in the Linkage Section must be equivalent to the definition of the corresponding parameter in the calling program. Thus DATE-STORE and INPUT-DATE, although they have different definitions, both consist of six characters of USAGE DISPLAY. They are thus equivalent.

The reason that the corresponding parameters must have equivalent definitions is because they occupy the same storage location. Thus no additional storage is allocated for INPUT-DATE — it is simply an automatic redefinition of DATE-STORE.

So when INPUT-DATE is referenced, the data in DATE-STORE is accessed. Similarly IN-DAY refers to the first two characters of DATE-STORE, etc.

The sequence of operations starting with the first statement shown in the Procedure Division of VALIDATION-CONTROL is

1.   the date is moved into the parameter DATE-STORE

2.   control is transferred by the CALL to the start of the Procedure Division of DATE-CHECK

3.   within this program the date in INPUT-DATE is validated

4.   if the date is valid, 0 is moved to ERROR-FLAG; if there is an error, 1 is moved to ERROR-FLAG

5.   EXIT PROGRAM returns control to the statement following the CALL

6.   the contents of ERROR-FLAG set up by DATE-CHECK are tested using the condition-name DATE-ERROR.

10.3   COMPARATIVE MERITS OF PERFORM AND CALL

At first glance the only thing the CALL statement seems to offer the programmer is more work. Compared to PERFORMing a paragraph, the programmer must write an extra Identification Division, Environment Division, two USING phrases and a Linkage Section. So what do we get in return for all this effort?

The major consideration used to be efficiency. Each program is compiled separately. So by splitting a large program into a number of small ones it is often possible to recompile only one or two small programs when changes have to be made. In addition with careful planning some of the called programs can be used in different run units.

A possibly more important consideration now is that splitting a run unit into separate programs is the best way of achieving independent modules. Unlike paragraphs it is impossible to branch into the middle of another module using GO TO (or PERFORM) and equally important, data in a module can be protected from corruption by another module.

10.4   SUMMARY

The following have been covered in this chapter

1.   CALL which transfers control to another program

2.   EXIT PROGRAM which returns control to the calling program

3.   The USING phrase which is used to list parameters in the CALL statement in the calling program and the Procedure Division header in the called program

4.   The Linkage Section which is used to define parameters in the called program

5.   The relative merits of CALL and PERFORM

QUIZ

1.   Assume you are required to write a subprogram called DATE-CONVERT which takes a date in the form YYMMDD and converts it to the form DD MMM YY. For example 811204 would become 4 DEC 81.

Produce the following coding

(a)   a CALL statement which would invoke DATE-CONVERT

(b)   a Linkage Section for DATE-CONVERT

(c)   a Procedure Division header for DATE-CONVERT

2.   Which verb, PERFORM or CALL, offers each of the following

(a)   better data protection

(b)   a mechanism for repeated execution of a module

(c)   parameters

(d)   separate compilation of modules

OTHER FEATURES

1.   **The CALL Identifier.**

The program executed by a particular CALL statement need not be decided until run time. If the verb CALL is followed by an identifier rather than a literal then the program whose name is stored in the identifier is executed.

```
eg   1     REQUIRED-CONVERTER PIC X(30).
           .
           .
           .
           .

           IF FULL-DATE-REQUIRED
              MOVE "CONVERT-TO-FULL-DATE" TO REQUIRED-CONVERTER
           ELSE
              MOVE "CONVERT-TO-SHORT-DATE" TO REQUIRED-CONVERTER
           END-IF
           CALL REQUIRED-CONVERTER USING . . .
```

2.   The CANCEL Statement

It might happen when a program is CALLed that there is insufficient central storage space available for it. This can be detected by using the ON EXCEPTION phrase of CALL. Space can then be released by "cancelling" a called program which is no longer required. This is done by using the CANCEL statement.

11 Sorting

It would be possible for us to write our own sort routine whenever we needed to sort a file. But because this would be extremely tedious COBOL provides a sort feature for us.

The file to be sorted can either be in existence before the sort begins or can be created by the program using what is known as an *input procedure*. The sorted file can either be output to backing store or can be handed over, a record at a time, for immediate processing by another part of the program known as an *output procedure*. Figure 11.1 shows the sort feature obtaining records from the input file or the input procedure, using the sort file for temporary storage during the sort, and outputting the sorted records to the output file or the output procedure.

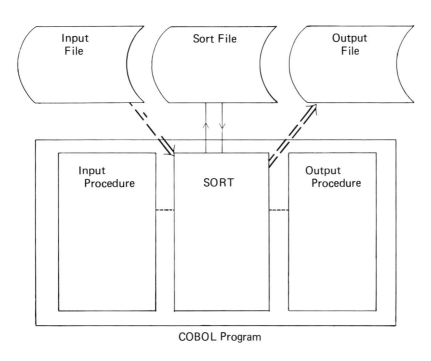

Figure 11.1 The Sort Feature

115

In this chapter we will look at how we specify the sequence into which the file is to be sorted. We will then see three examples of the sort feature in use.

11.1   SPECIFYING THE SEQUENCE

To introduce the terminology needed we take the example of a simple file containing four records. Each contains a salesman's code number, a sales value and a date in the form YYMMDD:

Salesman	Sales Value	Date
SMITH	146.21	810314
BROWN	153.10	810316
GREEN	498.23	810314
JONES	231.63	810313

If the records were sorted into descending sequence by sales value the result would be:

Salesman	Sales Value	Date
GREEN	498.23	810314
JONES	231.63	810313
BROWN	153.10	810316
SMITH	146.21	810314

The records have been resequenced so that the sales values appear in descending sequence.

We could instead sort the records into ascending sequence by salesman's name. Since the name is alphabetic this will imply alphabetical order:

Salesman	Sales Value	Date
BROWN	153.10	810316
GREEN	498.23	810314
JONES	231.63	810313
SMITH	146.21	810314

The data item used to determine the sequence (the sales value, and then the salesman's name in the above examples) is known as the *sort key*. We can have two keys — a *major key* which determines the overall sequence of the file and a *minor key* which determines the sequence of those records which have the same major key value. For example we could sort our simple file using date as the major key in ascending order, and sales value as the minor key in descending order.

Salesman	Sales Value	Date
JONES	231.63	810313
GREEN	498.23	810314
SMITH	146.21	810314
BROWN	153.10	810316

11.2   THE COBOL SORT FEATURE

When we want to sort a file in a COBOL program we use the SORT statement. It consists of the following components:

1.   the verb SORT

2.   the name of the sort file (used for temporary storage during the sort)

3.   a specification of the keys

4.   a specification of the source of the unsorted records

5.   a specification of the destination of the sorted records

Let us assume that we wish to do the sort indicated in figure 11.2.

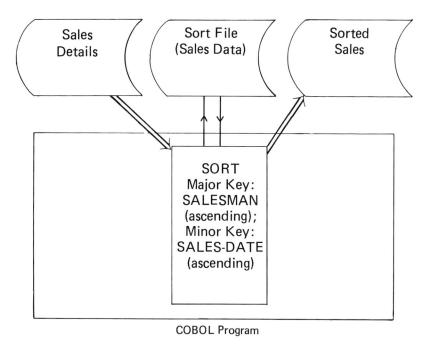

Figure 11.2   A Sort with Input File and Output File

The statement to do this sort appears in figure 11.3. It sorts the records in SALES-DETAILS into the sequence indicated by the ASCENDING KEY phrase and they are written to SORTED-SALES. The keys are listed in order of importance — the major key SALESMAN first and the minor key SALES-DATE last. (If more than two keys were used the other keys would appear, in order of significance, between the major key and the minor key.)

```
SORT SALES-DATA
   ON ASCENDING KEY SALESMAN
                        SALES-DATE
   USING SALES-DETAILS
   GIVING SORTED-SALES
```

Figure 11.3   A SORT Statement

SALES-DETAILS and SORTED-SALES are defined like any other files by means of Select and FD entries. Unlike other files, however, they must not be opened prior to the sort or closed after it. The SORT statement performs these functions automatically.

The sort file, in this case SALES-DATA, must be defined in a *sort description entry*. This consists of the indicator SD followed by the sort file name (as specified in the SORT statement) and optionally the RECORD CONTAINS and DATA RECORDS clauses (like those used in FD entries). It is followed by a description of the records being sorted (see figure 11.4).

```
DATA DIVISION.
FILE SECTION.
FD      SALES-DETAILS . . . .
1       SALES-DET-REC     PIC X(33).
FD      SORTED-SALES   . . . .
1       SORTED-SALES-REC PIC X(33).
SD      SALES-DATA.
1       SALES-REC.
   3       SALESMAN          PIC X(20).
   3       SALES-VALUE       PIC 9(5)V99.
   3       SALES-DATE        PIC 9(6).
             .
             .
             .

PROCEDURE DIVISION.
SORT-THE-SALES.
      SORT SALES-DATA
         ON ASCENDING KEY SALESMAN
                              SALES-DATE
         USING SALES-DETAILS
         GIVING SORTED-SALES
      STOP RUN.
```

Figure 11.4   A Sort Program

The sort record description must contain the keys being used in the sort — in this case SALESMAN and SALES-DATE. These data items are the ones which are referred to in the SORT statement.

All we need to do to make figure 11.4 into a complete program is to provide an Identification Division and an Environment Division. (Select entries are required for all three files. The one for the sort file may not contain any of the optional Select entry clauses.)

11.3   OUTPUT PROCEDURES

Let us now assume that instead of writing the sorted sales records to backing store we are going to use them to produce a sales report (see figure 11.5).

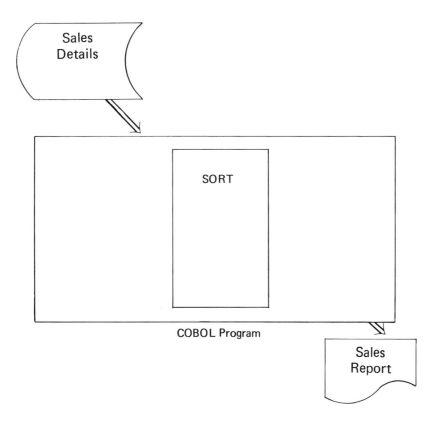

Figure 11.5   The Sales Report Program

This means that instead of writing the sorted records directly to a file they are going to be handed to an output procedure. This is indicated in the SORT statement as follows (where SALES-PRINT is the name of a paragraph in the program).

```
SORT SALES-DATA
    ON ASCENDING KEY SALESMAN
                     SALES-DATE
    USING SALES-DETAILS
    OUTPUT PROCEDURE IS SALES-PRINT
```

Within SALES-PRINT, records are obtained from the sort by executing the RETURN statement — in the same way as READ is executed to obtain records from a file. The process is represented in figure 11.6.

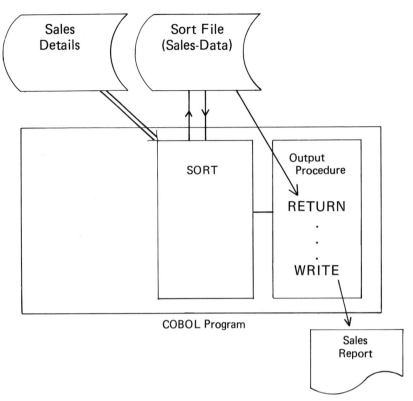

Figure 11.6   An Output Procedure

The SORT statement obtains the records from SALES-DETAILS and sorts them as in the previous example but in the final phase of the sort, instead of writing them to a file, it performs the output procedure. The output procedure is called once only (*not* once per record). It is the responsibility of the Output Procedure to obtain the sorted records by executing RETURN statements. The rest of the output procedure is just like any other routine for producing a printed report. When control drops out of the bottom of the output procedure it returns to the SORT statement (as if the section had been PERFORMed by the SORT).

Figure 11.7 shows the outline of the COBOL Procedure Division for this problem. The descriptions of the sort file and sort record are the same as in figure 11.4

```
SORT-SALES.
    SORT-SALES-DATA
        ON ASCENDING KEY SALESMAN
                         SALES-DATE
        USING SALES-DETAILS
        OUTPUT PROCEDURE IS SALES-PRINT.
    STOP RUN.


SALES-PRINT.
*initialise
    OPEN OUTPUT SALES-REPORT
    RETURN SALES-DATA
        AT END MOVE "Y" TO EOF-FLAG
    END-RETURN

*process records
*    process & RETURN sales records

*terminate
    CLOSE SALES-REPORT
```

Figure 11.7   An Output Procedure in COBOL

In this extract the RETURN statement shown will obtain the first record from the sort file. Subsequent executions of RETURN statements within this output procedure will obtain the records in sequence. (These subsequent RETURN statements are not shown in Figure 11.7.) Like the READ statement RETURN has an optional INTO phrase and a compulsory AT END phrase.

11.4 INPUT PROCEDURES

Let us now assume that instead of obtaining the records to be sorted directly from a file, we wish to produce them in an input procedure. Imagine that we wish to extract from an Order File those records with A or C stored in the Customer Code field, sort them into descending sequence by order value within ascending sequence by Customer Code and place them in another file (see figure 11.8).

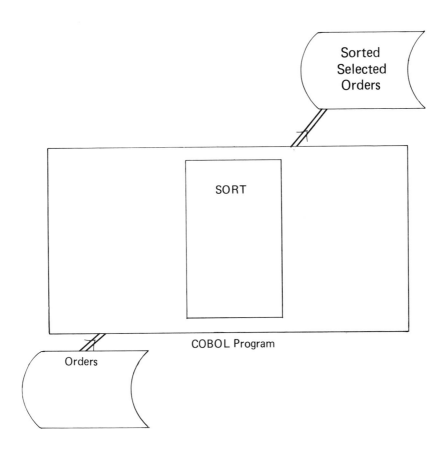

Figure 11.8 The Order Selection Program

We need an input procedure which will read the records from Orders File. For each record we must check if it is Customer Code A or C and if it is, hand it over to the sort. This "handing over" is done by means of the RELEASE statement (see figure 11.9).

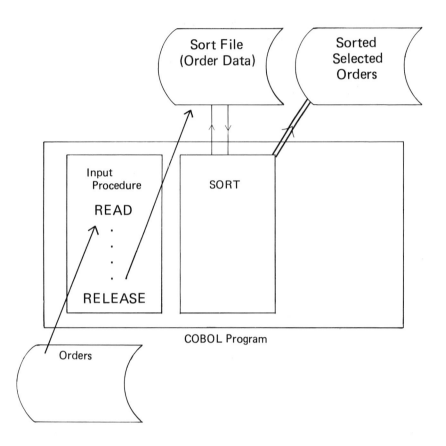

Figure 11.9   An Input Procedure

A sample Data Division and Procedure Division showing how this problem might be expressed in COBOL is shown in figure 11.10.

In this SORT statement you will notice that the major key is to be sorted in ascending sequence and the minor key into descending sequence. This is simply achieved by using two KEY phrases, the first one ASCENDING KEY, the second DESCENDING KEY. As required by the rules, the keys CUST-CODE and ORDER-VALUE are defined in the sort record (ORDER-DATA-REC).

When the SORT statement is executed it performs the input procedure, ORDER-SELECT-ION section, to obtain the records for sorting. The input procedure hands over the records for sorting one at a time by executing a RELEASE statement. The RELEASE statement, like WRITE, refers to the record-name (in the case of RELEASE the sort record name) and can optionally have a FROM phrase. When control drops out of the bottom of the input procedure, control returns to the SORT statement which proceeds to sort all the records which have been RELEASEd.

```
FILE SECTION.
FD      ORDERS-IN . . . .
1       ORDERS-IN-REC     PIC X(50).
FD      SELECTED-ORDERS . . .
1       SELECTED-ORD-REC PIC X(50).
SD      ORDER-DATA.
1       ORDER-DATA-REC.
   3    CUST-CODE          PIC X.
     88 CATEGORY-A                      VALUE "A".
     88 CATEGORY-C                      VALUE "C".
   3    ORDER-DATE         PIC 9(6).
   3    ORDER-VALUE        PIC 9(6)  COMP.
1       END-OF-FILE-FLAG PIC X.
     88 END-OF-FILE                     VALUE "Y".

                 .
                 .
                 .
                 .

PROCEDURE DIVISION.

SORT-ORDERS.
     SORT ORDER-DATA
          ON ASCENDING KEY CUST-CODE
          ON DESCENDING KEY ORDER-VALUE
          INPUT PROCEDURE ORDER-SELECTION
          GIVING SELECTED-ORDERS
     STOP RUN.

ORDER-SELECTION.

*initialise
     OPEN ORDERS-IN
     MOVE "N" TO END-OF-FILE-FLAG
     READ ORDERS-IN
       AT END MOVE "Y" TO END-OF-FILE-FLAG
     END-READ

*select records
     PERFORM UNTIL END-OF-FILE
          IF CATEGORY-A OR CATEGORY-C
          THEN
               RELEASE ORDER-DATA-REC
          END-IF
          READ ORDERS-IN
            AT END MOVE "Y" TO END-OF-FILE-FLAG
          END-READ
     END-PERFORM

*terminate
     CLOSE ORDERS-IN
```

Figure 11.10   An Input Procedure in COBOL

11.5   RULES FOR INPUT AND OUTPUT PROCEDURES

Each input or output procedure must be a paragraph or group of paragraphs. A group of consecutive paragraphs may be specified by writing

$$\begin{Bmatrix} \text{INPUT} \\ \text{OUTPUT} \end{Bmatrix} \underline{\text{PROCEDURE}} \text{ procedure-name-1 } \underline{\text{THROUGH}} \text{ procedure-name-2.}$$

Execution begins at the first statement in procedure-name-1 and control is returned to the SORT statement after executing the last statement in procedure-name-2.

11.6   SUMMARY

This chapter has introduced the terminology and concepts of file sorting in COBOL. The following COBOL statements were introduced and seen in use:

$$\underline{\text{SORT}} \text{ sort-file-name}$$
$$\begin{Bmatrix} \text{ON} \begin{Bmatrix} \underline{\text{ASCENDING}} \\ \underline{\text{DESCENDING}} \end{Bmatrix} \text{KEY data-name} \dots \end{Bmatrix} \dots$$
$$\begin{Bmatrix} \underline{\text{INPUT PROCEDURE}} \text{ is procedure-name-1 } [\underline{\text{THROUGH}} \text{ procedure-name-2}] \\ \underline{\text{USING}} \text{ file-name-1} \end{Bmatrix}$$
$$\begin{Bmatrix} \underline{\text{OUTPUT PROCEDURE}} \text{ is procedure-name-3 } [\underline{\text{THROUGH}} \text{ procedure-name-4}] \\ \underline{\text{GIVING}} \text{ file-name-2} \end{Bmatrix}$$
$$\underline{\text{RELEASE}} \text{ record-name } [\underline{\text{FROM}} \text{ identifier}]$$
$$\underline{\text{RETURN}} \text{ file-name } \underline{\text{RECORD}} \text{ } [\underline{\text{INTO}} \text{ identifier}]$$
$$\underline{\text{AT END}} \text{ imperative-statement}$$
$$\underline{\text{END-RETURN}}$$

QUIZ

1.   Consider the following SORT statement

    SORT AMENDMENTS

       ASCENDING KEY DATE BATCH-NO

       INPUT PROCEDURE VALIDATE-AMENDMENTS

       GIVING SORTED-AMENDMENTS

    (a)   What OPEN statements must be used for AMENDMENTS and SORTED-AMEND-MENTS?

    (b)   How many times is VALIDATE-AMENDMENTS executed for each execution of the SORT statement?

    (c)   Where else in the program will the name AMENDMENTS appear?

    (d)   What name must be specified in the RELEASE statements in VALIDATE-AMEND-MENTS?

    (e)   Under what circumstances would a RETURN be used in VALIDATE-AMENDMENTS?

    (f)   Can VALIDATE-AMENDMENTS be a paragraph-name?

    (g)   If the following records were released to the sort in what order would they be output to SORTED-AMENDMENTS?

BATCH-NO	DATE	Details
05	810416	ABC..
06	810417	DEF..
04	810416	GHI..
07	810415	JKL..
06	810417	MNO..

OTHER FEATURES

1. Multiple Input Files

If the records that are to be sorted are stored in more than one file they can be combined and sorted by using a single SORT statement. All that is necessary is to list all the files in the USING phrase:

    USING file-name-1, file-name-2 etc

2. Merging

When two or more files are in the same sequences, by the same keys (in the same positions in the records) they can be merged into one file by using the MERGE statement. For example

```
MERGE SALES-DATA

    ASCENDING KEY IS SALESMAN

    DESCENDING KEY IS SALES-VALUE

    USING JAN-SALES FEB-SALES MAR-SALES

    GIVING FIRST-QUARTER-SALES
```

As with the SORT, SALES-DATA must be defined in an SD entry and a SELECT entry and the keys must be defined in the record following the SD entry. An output procedure may be specified but input procedures may not.

The same effect would result if a SORT statement of the same format had been used in place of the MERGE above but by using the MERGE the compiler can take advantage of the fact that the input files are in the correct sequence and the desired result is achieved far more efficiently.

12 Indexed Files

So far we have only processed files sequentially — starting at the beginning and progressing through each record in turn. You read a novel this way — starting at page 1 and progressing through each page in turn. However you read a COBOL text book somewhat differently. Sometimes when you pick up the book you will want to go straight to the start of, say, chapter 12. Other times you might want to go straight to the page where the rules of PERFORM are. In neither case would it be acceptable to read the book from page 1 until you find what you are looking for. In other words you need some form of direct access and in the case of the rules for PERFORM you need an index.

The same requirements exist with files. Imagine that an order clerk at a builders merchants is sitting at a terminal and wants to find out whether there are enough cases of mottled brown kitchen tiles in stock. It would be unacceptable for the clerk to have to wait while the computer read a few thousand stock records looking for the one for mottled brown kitchen tiles. Instead, the way it could be done is to have a unique key value associated with each stock record: a stock code number. The file would have an index containing the key values and the address on the disk where the record for each key is stored.

Files such as these are known as *indexed* files. In a COBOL program you can specify a key value and then issue a read statement which will automatically look up the index and obtain the required record. The index is set up automatically when the file is first created and is amended automatically when the file is subsequently altered. So the programmer doesn't have to worry about the index at all.

With indexed files it is possible to read the records in ascending sequence by key value — this is known as *sequential access*. It is also possible to read the records in any other desired order — this is known as *random access*.

In this chapter we will see how to
- — define an indexed file
- — create an indexed file
- — read an indexed file randomly
- — read an indexed file sequentially

12.1   DEFINING INDEXED FILES

Indexed files, like all other files, are defined using a Select entry, a File Description entry and record descriptions. The file description entails no new clauses and the record description differs from other files only in that you must define the data item which is used as the key: to identify the record. In figure 12.1 STOCK-CODE is the key.

```
SELECT STOCK-FILE ASSIGN SF378
    ORGANIZATION IS INDEXED
    ACCESS MODE IS SEQUENTIAL
    RECORD KEY IS STOCK-CODE.
        .
        .
        .
        .

FD    STOCK-FILE . . . . . .
1     STOCK-RECORD.
    3 STOCK-DESCRIPTION   PIC X(30).
    3 STOCK-CODE          PIC X(6).
    3 STOCK-LEVEL         PIC 9(5).
    3 UNIT-COST           PIC 9(4)V99.
```

Figure 12.1   Definition of an Indexed File

The Select entry does have some new clauses in it. First we must specify

ORGANIZATION IS INDEXED

to indicate that it is an indexed file. Secondly, since we can access the file sequentially or randomly, we will need the Access Mode clause. We write

ACCESS MODE IS SEQUENTIAL

or   ACCESS MODE IS RANDOM

depending on the type of access required for the file in this program. Finally we must indicate which data item in the file's record description contains the key. We do this by writing

RECORD KEY IS data-name

where data-name must be the data item in the associated record description which is used as the key. In figure 12.1 it is STOCK-CODE.

12.2   CREATION OF INDEXED FILES

Creating an indexed file is very similar to creating a sequential file. The file is opened for output, the records are written and then the file is closed. The only differences are

1.   the records must be written in ascending sequence by the key values, using the WRITE statement with the INVALID KEY option.

2.   the Select entry must contain the correct Organisation, Access Mode and Record Key clauses. In this case we must have ACCESS MODE IS SEQUENTIAL since we are processing the file in key sequence.

Figure 12.2 shows the outline of a program to create a stock-file with indexed organisation.

```
      SELECT STOCK-FILE ASSIGN SF378
          ORGANIZATION IS INDEXED
          ACCESS MODE IS SEQUENTIAL
          RECORD KEY IS STOCK-CODE.
                 .
                 .
                 .
                 .
  FD   STOCK-FILE . . . .
  1    STOCK-RECORD.
    3  STOCK-DESCRIPTION PIC X(30).
    3  STOCK-CODE        PIC X(6).
    3  STOCK-LEVEL       PIC 9(5).
    3  UNIT-COST         PIC 9(4)V99.
                 .
                 .
                 .
                 .

      OPEN OUTPUT STOCK-FILE
      for each stock record
        set up stock record including STOCK-CODE
        WRITE STOCK-RECORD
          INVALID KEY PERFORM SEQ-ERROR
        END-WRITE
      CLOSE STOCK-FILE
```

Figure 12.2   Creation of an Indexed File

The records are written one after the other and the key value is extracted from the records and used to set up an index. This is completely automatic — all the programmer must do is get the definition right and output the records in ascending sequence.

If the records are not in ascending sequence the imperative-statement following INVALID KEY (in the WRITE statement) is executed.

12.3   RANDOM READING

In COBOL the term random access is used when records are accessed in any order other than the order in which they are stored in the file. It is the alternative to sequential access.

The definition will be the same as when the file was created except that we must now specify ACCESS MODE IS RANDOM in the Select entry. In the Procedure Division, to do a random read we must first move the key value of the required record into the RECORD KEY data item and then execute a read statement.

The read statement differs from the ones used so far in that it has an INVALID KEY phrase. The format is

READ file-name RECORD [INTO identifier]

INVALID KEY statement-1 ...

END-READ

The imperative statement is executed when a record with the specified key cannot be found. Figure 12.3 shows an example of a random read.

```
                    SELECT STOCK-FILE ASSIGN SF378
                        ORGANIZATION IS INDEXED
                        ACCESS MODE IS RANDOM
                        RECORD KEY IS STOCK-CODE.
                            .
                            .
                            .
                            .

          FD    STOCK-FILE . . . .
          1     STOCK-RECORD.
                3 STOCK-DESCRIPTION PIC X(30).
                3 STOCK-CODE        PIC X(6).
                3 STOCK-LEVEL       PIC 9(5).
                3 UNIT-COST         PIC 9(4)V99.
                            .
                            .
                            .
                            .

                    OPEN INPUT STOCK-FILE
                            .
                            .
                            .

          *     reqd-key contains the key
          *     of the required record
                MOVE REQD-KEY TO STOCK-CODE
                MOVE "Y" TO RECORD-FOUND
                READ STOCK-FILE
                    INVALID KEY MOVE "N" TO RECORD-FOUND
                END-READ
                IF RECORD-FOUND = "N"
                THEN
                    PERFORM REPORT-MISSING-RECORD
                ELSE
                    PERFORM PROCESS-RECORD
                END-READ
                            .
                            .
                            .
                            .

                    CLOSE STOCK-FILE
```

Figure 12.3   Random Read of an Indexed File

12.4 SEQUENTIAL READING

An indexed file can be read sequentially like any other file. The Select entry must contain the ORGANIZATION INDEXED, ACCESS SEQUENTIAL and RECORD KEY clauses and in the Procedure Division the normal READ with the AT END branch is used.

However, unlike sequential files, you do not have to start reading at the beginning of the file. You can start with any record. To indicate the key value of the record you wish to start at, you use the START statement whose simplest format is

<u>START</u> file name

    <u>INVALID</u> KEY statement-1 ...

<u>END-START</u>

With the Stock File we could move the required key to the record key (STOCK-CODE) and then execute START STOCK-FILE. We could then start reading from the record in the file with that key value by using a succession of normal READ statements (see figure 12.4).

```
        SELECT STOCK-FILE ASSIGN SF378
            ORGANIZATION IS INDEXED
            ACCESS MODE IS SEQUENTIAL
            RECORD KEY IS STOCK-CODE.
                  .
                  .
                  .
    FD  STOCK-FILE . . . .
    1   STOCK-RECORD.
        3 STOCK-DESCRIPTION PIC X(30).
        3 STOCK-CODE        PIC X(6).
        3 STOCK-LEVEL       PIC 9(5).
        3 UNIT-COST         PIC 9(4)V99.
                  .
                  .
                  .
                  .
        OPEN INPUT STOCK-FILE.
                  .
                  .
                  .
    *   first-key contains the key of the
    *   record at which reading is to begin
        MOVE FIRST-KEY TO STOCK-CODE
        MOVE "Y" TO RECORD-FOUND
        START STOCK-FILE
            INVALID KEY MOVE "N" TO RECORD-FOUND
        END-START
        IF RECORD-FOUND = "N"
        THEN
            PERFORM REPORT-MISSING-RECORD
        ELSE
            READ STOCK-FILE
                AT END MOVE "Y" TO END-FILE
            END-READ
        END-IF
                  .
                  .
                  .
```

Figure 12.4 Sequential Read after START

In the example in figure 12.4 the file is positioned on the record with the key value stored in FIRST-KEY. The READ statement shown then reads the record with this value, and subsequent READs will each obtain the next record in sequence. The statement following INVALID KEY in the START statement will be executed if no record with the specified key exists on the file.

If the START statement was omitted the first READ would access the record with the lowest key value.

12.5 SUMMARY

In this chapter we have covered

  - The Select Entry for Indexed Files including the ORGANIZATION, ACCESS MODE and RECORD KEY clauses

  - Creation of Indexed Files

  - Random Reading of Indexed Files

  - Sequential Reading of Indexed Files

  - The START statement

QUIZ

1. Which Select Entry clauses (in addition to those used for Sequential files) are needed for processing Indexed files?

2. If an Indexed file starts with records having key values 5 6 13 19 22 which would be the second record read if

    (a) the file was read sequentially?

    (b) the file was read randomly?

3. Give a reason why the INVALID KEY clause might be executed in each of the following cases:

    (a) when used with a WRITE statement which is creating an indexed file

    (b) when used with a READ statement which is doing a random read

    (c) when used with a START statement.

OTHER FEATURES

1. START with KEY Option

Earlier in this chapter we saw the simplest form of START — where a record was sought with its record key value equal to a specified value. It is also possible to

    (i) start at the first record with a key value greater than a specified value

        eg START STOCK-FILE KEY GREATER THAN STOCK-CODE

    (ii) start at the first record with a key value which is not less than (ie greater than or equal to) a specified value

        eg START STOCK-FILE KEY NOT LESS THAN STOCK-CODE

(iii) perform any of these matches (equal, greater than, not less than) on leading characters of the key. The example below is of an Invoice File in which the record key is INVOICE-NUMB. INVOICE-NUMB starts with the year and month in which the invoice was produced (YEAR-AND-MONTH) and finishes with a four digit sequence number. The program is required to print all invoices for the month indicated by REQD-YEAR-AND-MONTH.

```
FD   INVOICE-FILE . . .
1       INVOICE-REC.
   3    INVOICE-NUMB.
     5 YEAR-AND-MONTH PIC X(4).
     5 SEQUENCE-NUMB  PIC 9(4).
   3   . . . .
            .
            .
            .
            .

*    read invoices for month stored
*    in reqd-year-and-month
     MOVE REQD-YEAR-AND-MONTH TO YEAR-AND-MONTH
     START INVOICE-FILE KEY = YEAR-AND-MONTH
        INVALID KEY MOVE "N" TO RECORD-FOUND
     END-START
            .
            .
            .
            .
```

The effect of the START statement is to locate the first record with the specified year and month number. The next READ statement will then retrieve this record. Each subsequent READ will obtain the next record in sequence.

2.   Dynamic Access

It is possible to mix random and sequential access of an indexed file. To do this ACCESS IS DYNAMIC must be specified in the Select entry. Random READs are performed exactly as when ACCESS IS RANDOM is specified. For sequential accesses you must write

READ file-name NEXT . . .

The word NEXT indicates that the next record in sequence is to be read.

3.   Alternate Keys

In addition to accessing records through the record key value it is also possible to access them through other keys. If, when the file is created, the clause

ALTERNATE RECORD KEY IS data-name

is specified, a second index is automatically set up using the value in the specified data-name. This index can be used subsequently to directly access the records. Like the main index (which contains record key values) this index is maintained automatically so the programmer need not even be aware of its existence. Unlike the record key the same alternate record key value may be used in more than one record in the file.

To access a record with the key value stored in an alternate key called STOCK-TYPE you would write

```
READ STOCK-FILE
    KEY IS STOCK-TYPE
    INVALID KEY . . . .
```

More than one alternate key may be specified if desired so an indexed file may be accessed using any number of different keys. Sequential access is however only possible using the record key (not an alternate key).

13   File Updating

The Stock File we processed in the last chapter is an example of a *master* file – that is a file which shows the current state of some aspect of an organisation's activities. The Stock File shows what items are in stock and the level of stock for each item. We saw how to create the file and then how to read it. There would however be little point in reading it if it was not kept up to date with changes to the stock levels, addition of new stock items and the deletion of those no longer stocked.

This need to update applies to any master file – an employees file in a public utility, a suppliers file in a retail company and a customer accounts file in a bank. We shall use the last example to illustrate the principles of file updating in COBOL. Let us assume for the sake of simplicity that each record contains the account number, the current balance of the account and the name of the account, say:

```
1   ACCOUNT-RECORD.

  3 ACCOUNT-NUM    PIC 9(8).

  3 BALANCE        PIC 9(6)V99.

  3 ACCOUNT-NAME   PIC X(30).
```

There are three types of changes (or *transactions*) we will need to make to this file. They are

(1)   Amendments: changes to contents of a record (eg change of account-name)

(2)   Deletions: the deletion of an existing record (when an account is closed)

(3)   Insertions: the insertion of a new record (when a new account is opened)

Two distinct approaches to updating are possible in COBOL. One is *father-son* updating where a completely new copy of the master file is made everytime it is updated. The second is updating *in place* where the alterations are made to the existing copy of the master file. We will now look at each of these more carefully using our example of the Accounts File.

13.1   FATHER-SON UPDATE

For this method of update the transactions must be sorted into the same sequence as the accounts file. The old accounts file and the transaction file are read together in sequence – all the changes are made in the computer's store and a completely new accounts file is created (see figure 13.1).

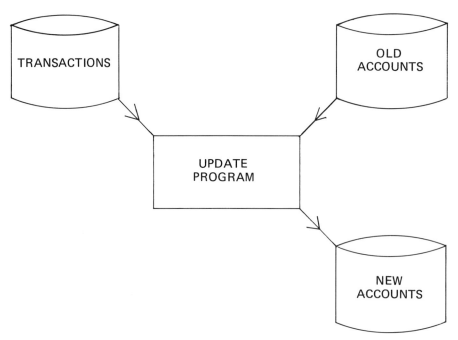

Figure 13.1 A Father-Son Update

Since only sequential processing is involved the files can have Sequential or Indexed Organisation. The method works equally well on any magnetic media (tape or disk). No new COBOL features are required. The only thing that is new is the logic in the Procedure Division needed to make the desired alterations. A discussion of this logic can be found in books on program design. An outline of the COBOL features used is shown in figure 13.2.

```
FD   OLD-ACCOUNT-FILE . . .
1    OLD-ACCOUNT-RECORD.
  3 OLD-ACCOUNT-NUMB  PIC 9(8).
  3 OLD-BALANCE       PIC 9(6)V99.
  3 OLD-ACCOUNT-NAME  PIC X(30).
FD   NEW-ACCOUNT-FILE . . .
1    NEW-ACCOUNT-RECORD.
  3 NEW-ACCOUNT-NUMB  PIC 9(8).
  3 NEW-BALANCE       PIC 9(6)V99.
  3 NEW-ACCOUNT-NUMB  PIC X(30).
                 .
                 .
                 .
                 .

     OPEN INPUT OLD-ACCOUNT-FILE
     OPEN INPUT TRANSACTION-FILE
     OPEN OUTPUT NEW-ACCOUNT-FILE
     READ OLD-ACCOUNT-FILE . . .
     READ TRANSACTION-FILE . . .
                 .
                 .
                 .

     IF AMENDMENT
        MOVE OLD-ACCOUNT-RECORD TO NEW-ACCOUNT-RECORD
        Make all the changes
        WRITE NEW-ACCOUNT-RECORD
```

```
            .
            .
            .
            .
IF DELETION
   write nothing to NEW-ACCOUNT-FILE
   and move onto next account
      .

      .

      .
IF INSERTION
   use transaction to set up new record
   in NEW-ACCOUNT-RECORD
   WRITE NEW-ACCOUNT-RECORD
      .
      .
      .
      .
```

Figure 13.2   Outline of a Father-Son Update in COBOL

13.2   UPDATING IN PLACE

The father-son update is inefficient when only a few changes are made in an update run and, for all but the smallest files, it is completely impractical for on-line applications. In these the transactions come in one at a time and they must be used to update the files before the next transaction is processed. In such cases we must have just one copy of the master file and we must change it for each transaction (see figure 13.3).

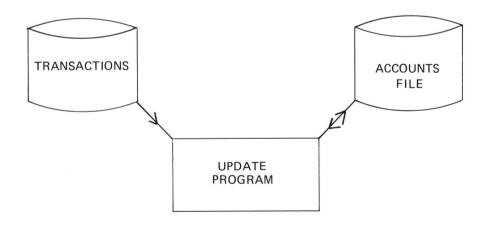

Figure 13.3   Updating in Place

With this approach

1.   amendments are handled by reading in the relevant account record, making changes to it in store and writing the amended record using the REWRITE verb.

2.   deletions are handled by executing the DELETE verb.

3.   insertions are handled by inserting a new record using the WRITE verb.

Since there is only one accounts file we only need one FD entry and since we are transferring records to and from it we must open it in the input-output mode, ie

OPEN I-O ACCOUNT-FILE.

13.3   UPDATING IN PLACE – SEQUENTIAL FILES

Some limited updating in place is possible with sequentially organised files: amendments are possible using the REWRITE verb (see figure 13.4).

```
FD   ACCOUNT-FILE . . . .
1    ACCOUNT-RECORD.
  3 ACCOUNT-NUMB PIC 9(8).
  3 BALANCE       PIC 9(6)V99.
  3 ACCOUNT-NAME PIC X(30).
                  .
                  .
                  .
                  .

  OPEN I-O ACCOUNT-FILE
  OPEN INPUT TRANSACTION-FILE

                  .
                  .
                  .
                  .

  READ ACCOUNT-FILE
  IF changes for this record
    make the changes to ACCOUNT-RECORD
    REWRITE ACCOUNT-RECORD
  END-IF
```

Figure 13.4   Amending a File with REWRITE

The Accounts file is opened in I-O mode and its records are read in sequence; when amendments exist for a record, the ACCOUNT-RECORD is changed accordingly and the new version of the record is stored on top of the old one by executing a REWRITE statement. The action of the REWRITE is to store the record in the specified record area on top of the last record read from that file.

With sequential files it is not possible to delete records although there is nothing to stop the programmer from Rewriting a record which contains an indication that an Account has been closed. Obviously all programs reading that file would have to check the indicator before processing each record.

It is also impossible to insert new records in the middle of a sequential file. They can only be added to the end – using OPEN EXTEND.

13.4   UPDATING IN PLACE – INDEXED FILES

In indexed files all three types of transaction are catered for. An example is shown in figure 13.5.

```
           SELECT ACCOUNT-FILE ASSIGN AC131
              ORGANIZATION IS INDEXED
              ACCESS MODE IS RANDOM
              RECORD KEY IS ACCOUNT-NUMB.
           SELECT TRANSACTION-FILE ASSIGN TR148
                 .
                 .
                 .

FD     ACCOUNT-FILE . . . .
1      ACCOUNT-RECORD.
 3     ACCOUNT-NUMB PIC 9(8).
 3     BALANCE      PIC 9(6)V99.
 3     ACCOUNT-NAME PIC X(30).
FD     TRANSACTION-FILE . . .
1      TRANS-RECORD.
 3     TRANS-CODE    PIC 9.
   88 AMENDMENT              VALUE 1.
   88 DELETION               VALUE 2.
   88 INSERTION              VALUE 3.
 3     TRANS-AC-NO  PIC 9(8).
              .
              .
 3            .
              .

       OPEN I-0 ACCOUNT-FILE
       OPEN INPUT TRANSACTION-FILE
              .
              .
              .

       READ TRANSACTION-FILE . . .

       IF AMENDMENT
          MOVE TRANS-AC-NO TO ACCOUNT-NUMB
          READ ACCOUNT-FILE INVALID KEY . . .
          make changes to ACCOUNT-RECORD
          REWRITE ACCOUNT-RECORD INVALID KEY . . . .

       IF DELETION
          MOVE TRANS-AC-NO TO ACCOUNT-NUMB
          DELETE ACCOUNT-FILE RECORD INVALID KEY . . . .

       IF INSERTION
          MOVE TRANS-AC-NO TO ACCOUNT-NUMB
          set up rest of ACCOUNT-RECORD
          WRITE ACCOUNT-RECORD INVALID KEY . . . .
```

Figure 13.5   Updating an Indexed File Randomly

The transaction file, which may be in any order, is read sequentially. Each record on the transaction file is an amendment, a deletion or an insertion.

For amendments the required record is read from the accounts file by means of a random read. The alterations are made to ACCOUNT-RECORD and the record is rewritten. When used with Random Access Mode the REWRITE will write the record to the file on top of the record which has the key value stored in ACCOUNT-NUMB (the record key) at the time the REWRITE is executed. In normal use this would be the record last read. The INVALID KEY clause is executed if no record with the specified key value exists.

For deletions the key value is transferred from the transaction record to the account record and then the DELETE statement is executed. The action of the DELETE statement is to remove from the file the record with the key value equal to the current value of the record key (in our case ACCOUNT-NUMB). If no such record exists the INVALID KEY phrase is executed. Once a record has been deleted it is no longer possible to read it.

For insertions the information in the transaction is used to set up a new ACCOUNT-RECORD including the key value. A WRITE statement is then executed to store the record in the file. This will cause the record to be inserted in the correct logical position in the file. The INVALID KEY phrase is executed if a record with the specified key value already exists on the file.

Any indexes are updated automatically when the DELETE and WRITE statements are executed.

13.5   SUMMARY

In this chapter we have looked at

- the principles of file updating
- father-son updating
- updating in place — sequential and indexed files

  OPEN I-O statement

  REWRITE statement

  DELETE statement

QUIZ

1. What statements are used for the following purposes when randomly updating a file?

 (a) opening the file

 (b) amending an existing record

 (c) deleting an existing record

 (d) creating a new record

2. What difference is there in the transaction file when doing a sequential rather than a random update?

3. Give one circumstance under which the INVALID KEY phrase will be executed with

 (a) REWRITE

 (b) DELETE

 (c) WRITE

OTHER FEATURES

1. Relative Files

A relative file is one where each record in the file is given an integral value. The first is 1, the second 2, and so on.

The file is described with a Select entry such as

```
SELECT PAY-FILE ASSIGN PF193
    ORGANIZATION IS RELATIVE
    ACCESS MODE IS RANDOM
    RELATIVE KEY IS PAYMENT-NO.
```

Unlike the record key in indexed files the relative key (PAYMENT-NO above) must *not* be defined in the file's record area. It is used to store the position in which a record is to be stored. For example, if we wanted to store the PAY-FILE record (PAY-RECORD, say) in position 1, we would use the following coding

```
MOVE 1 TO PAYMENT-NO
WRITE PAY-RECORD INVALID KEY . . .
```

Similarly to read the record in position 2 we would write

```
MOVE 2 TO PAYMENT-NO
READ PAY-FILE INVALID KEY . . .
```

Relative files can be processed in most of the ways that indexed files are, including the use of DELETE, REWRITE and START. The main difference is that alternate keys are not permitted.

2. The FILE STATUS Clause

A two character data item can be specified to receive an indication of the success or otherwise of input and output statements. The data item is defined in the FILE STATUS clause in the Select entry. When an exception occurs (of the type that causes the execution of the AT END or INVALID KEY clause) a code number indicating the nature of the exception is stored in the File Status data item. The programmer can thus discover the precise nature of the exception by examining this data item.

14 String Handling

So far we have confined our attention to data stored in fixed length data items which are in turn stored in fixed length records. These constraints have been imposed not because data and records are naturally fixed length, but because it is more convenient to handle fixed length items on computers.

Sometimes for the sake of efficiency or human acceptability we wish to override these constraints. In the next chapter we see examples of files containing records of more than one length. In this chapter we look at data items which are naturally variable in length. In fact most data is variable in length before the systems analyst regiments it. We are going to process names and addresses in their natural form:

> J. A. SMITH, 3 SALT ROAD, . . .

and P. V. W. MUSSELBOROUGH, 185 MOUNT HERIOT CRESCENT, . . .

rather than the fixed length equivalent

J . A . S M I T H	3 S A L T . . .
P . V . W . M U S S E L B O R O U G H	1 8 5 M O U . . .

or even the coded equivalent

employee number | 4 6 3 8 4 |

and | 1 4 9 3 2 |

Likewise we shall look at dates in the form

> 6 MAY 1981

> 13 SEPTEMBER 1981

rather than

810506

810913

To process data in this more natural form we have three statements in COBOL. They are

INSPECT which can scan a data item identifying any given string of characters and count how many times it occurs, or replace it with another string;

UNSTRING which splits a string of characters up into a number of smaller strings;

STRING which combines a number of strings into one larger string.

We will look at each of these in turn.

14.1   THE INSPECT STATEMENT

The INSPECT statement has two basic forms:

INSPECT with TALLYING which counts the number of occurrences of a string in a data item

INSPECT with REPLACING which replaces occurrences of a given string with another given string.

Assume that the data item

1 NAME-AND-ADDRESS PIC X(30)

contains the following data

```
 J . A . S M I T H , 3   S A L T   R D . ,    B R I S T O L
```

We can count the number of commas by writing

INSPECT NAME-AND-ADDRESS

   TALLYING LINE-COUNT FOR ALL ","

This would count the number of occurrences of "," in NAME-AND-ADDRESS and add the result to LINE-COUNT. So after executing the above statement LINE-COUNT would contain 2 (assuming it originally contained 0).

If we wished to count how many characters appear before the first comma and add the count to NAME-LENGTH we would write

INSPECT NAME-AND-ADDRESS

   TALLYING NAME-LENGTH FOR CHARACTERS

      BEFORE INITIAL ","

This will start at the beginning of NAME-AND-ADDRESS and will scan to the first "," counting how many characters occur. The result, in this case 9, is added to NAME-LENGTH.

If we wished to replace everything after the first comma by spaces we would write

INSPECT NAME—AND—ADDRESS

  REPLACING CHARACTERS BY SPACE

    AFTER FIRST ","

The result of this statement on our example data is

```
J . A . S M I T H ,
```

Many other variations are possible. For example you can

— search for a string of any length (not just one character) identified by a non-numeric literal or an identifier

— the replacement string can be any length, also expressed as a non-numeric literal or identifier

— when searching for a string (rather than CHARACTERS) the search can be for *all* occurrences of the STRING or just *leading* occurrences. In the case of replacement it can just be the *first* occurrence of the string

— whether tallying or replacing, the starting point or the ending point of the search can be specified by means of the BEFORE/AFTER phrase.

14.2 THE UNSTRING STATEMENT

This statement is used to split a string of characters into separate substrings. In its simplest form you write

    UNSTRING name-of-data-item-containing-string

    DELIMITED BY delimiter

    INTO name-of-first-substring

        name-of-second-substring

        etc.

Let us assume that we want to split up

1 NAME—AND—ADDRESS PIC X(30).

into three data items, NAME, ADDRESS(1) and ADDRESS (2):

```
1   FIXED—FORMAT—N—AND—A.
  3 NAME          PIC X(15).
  3 ADDRESS       PIC X(15) OCCURS 2.
```

with all the data before the first comma going into NAME, all the data between the first and second commas going in ADDRESS (1) and all the data between the second comma and third comma (or the end of NAME-AND-ADDRESS) going in ADDRESS (2). We would write

```
UNSTRING NAME-AND-ADDRESS
   DELIMITED BY ","
   INTO NAME
         ADDRESS (1)
         ADDRESS (2)
```

If NAME-AND-ADDRESS contained

```
J . A . S M I T H , 3   S A L T   R D . , B R I S T O L
```

the result of executing the above UNSTRING statement would be

```
J . A . S M I T H
```

```
3   S A L T   R D .
```

```
B R I S T O L
```

Additional facilities exist with UNSTRING to

— specify a delimiter of any length as a non-numeric literal or an identifier

— specify more than one delimiter

— count the number of characters moved into each data item

— start the unstring operation part way through a data item by setting a pointer to the first character to be processed.

14.3   THE STRING STATEMENT

This statement, as you might expect, is the reverse of UNSTRING. It combines separate strings into one larger string.

To demonstrate the statement let us assume we want to set up the date in a data item called THE-DATE in the form

THE-DATE:
```
T U E S D A Y ,   2 7   M A Y   1 9 8 0
```

and that currently the day of the week is already in position and the other data is stored as follows

DAY-NUMBER:
```
2 7
```

MONTH-NAME:
```
M A Y * * * * * *
```

YEAR:
```
8 0
```

Firstly we must set a pointer to the position in THE-DATE where the next character is to be moved in:

DATE-POSN

THE DATE | T U E S D A Y |

DATE-POSN is a normal numeric data item which currently contains 8. It could have been set to that value by INSPECTing for characters before the initial space (and adding 1) or, as you will shortly see, by moving the day of week (TUESDAY in this case) in with a STRING statement.

To move in the comma and space we write

> STRING
>
> ", " DELIMITED BY SIZE
>
> INTO THE-DATE
>
> WITH POINTER DATE-POSN

DELIMITED BY SIZE simply means move the whole literal ", ". The statement thus means move ", " into THE-DATE starting in the position indicated by DATE-POSN. After executing the statement, the pointer, DATE-POSN, will contain the location of the next available position, 10 in this case. So we have

DATE-POSN

| T U E S D A Y , |

To move in the day of the month we write

> STRING
>
> DAY-NUMBER DELIMITED BY SIZE
>
> INTO THE-DATE
>
> WITH POINTER DATE-POSN

The effect of the statement is

DATE-POSN

| T U E S D A Y ,   2 7 |

To move in the month we write

> STRING
>
> MONTH-NAME DELIMITED BY "*"
>
> INTO THE-DATE
>
> WITH POINTER DATE-POSN

This causes the contents of MONTH-NAME up to but excluding the first asterisk to be transferred into THE-DATE starting at the position indicated by DATE-POSN:

Finally we can move in the space, the century number and the year number all in one go by writing

STRING

   " 19" YEAR DELIMITED BY SIZE

   INTO THE-DATE

   WITH POINTER DATE-POSN

The second line indicates that " 19" and YEAR are to be moved in one after the other, both delimited by SIZE. This gives

```
                                                    DATE-POSN
                                                        |
| T U E S D A Y ,   2 7   M A Y   1 9 8 0 '           |         |
```

As with UNSTRING the delimiter can be a string of any length specified as a non-numeric literal or an identifier.

It is also possible to combine the above example into one STRING statement:

STRING

   ", " DELIMITED BY SIZE

   DAY-NUMBER DELIMITED BY SIZE

   MONTH-NAME DELIMITED BY "*"

   " 19" YEAR DELIMITED BY SIZE

   INTO THE-DATE

   WITH POINTER DATE-POSN

If the POINTER phrase is omitted the first character to be moved in will go to position 1, the beginning of the destination field. Unlike MOVE only the characters which are explicitly overwritten are affected by an execution of a STRING statement. For example, the last six characters of THE-DATE would contain whatever characters were there at the start. In our example they happen to be spaces.

14.4 SUMMARY

We have seen how COBOL handles data which is stored as variable text rather than fixed length data items. The three statements discussed were

INSPECT which scans a data item

   —   counting occurrences of a specified string, or

   —   replacing each occurrence of a given string by another string

UNSTRING which identifies delimiters in a data item and copies the strings between the delimiters into separate data items

STRING which combines separate strings into one data item

QUIZ

1. Study the following definition

    1   INPUT-VALUE   PIC X(5).

    1   SIGN-FLAG   PIC 9.

       88 VALUE-NEGATIVE   VALUE 1.

    INPUT-VALUE contains a right justified integer possibly with a minus sign. All the unused leading positions are occupied by spaces — eg

		—	4	3

    Use INSPECT statements to set condition-name VALUE-NEGATIVE to true if the minus sign is present and to replace any leading spaces and minus sign by zeros.

2. Use the STRING statement to combine SURNAME and FIRST-INITIAL into NAME as illustrated below

    SURNAME

J	O	N	E	S					

    FIRST-INITIAL

P

    NAME

J	O	N	E	S	,		P	.			

3. Write an UNSTRING statement to split NAME up into SURNAME and FIRST-INITIAL as illustrated in the previous question.

OTHER FEATURES

All three statements covered in this chapter have many variations not illustrated in the chapter. Some of these variations were mentioned briefly but others were not.

For example a single INSPECT statement can count several different character strings simultaneously and also replace several other character strings. It is likely that you will never use the full power of INSPECT. For the time being it is more important that you understand the basic capabilities of the three statements. A detailed study of their more exotic facilities could be delayed until a need arises for their use.

15 Variable Length Records

Back in chapter 5 we introduced the concept of two different types of record on the same file — in that case a meter reading record and a fault record:

```
FD    METER-READINGS LABEL RECORDS STANDARD.
1     METER-READINGS-REC.
  3   RECORD-CODE      PIC X.
  3   ACCOUNT-NO       PIC 9(8).
  3   METER-CODE       PIC X(5).
  3   METER-RDG-DATE.
    5 MTR-RDG-DAY      PIC 99.
    5 MTR-RDG-MONTH    PIC 99.
    5 MTR-RDG-YEAR     PIC 99.
  3   ACTUAL-READING   PIC 9(6).
1     METER-FAULT-REC.
  3   FILLER           PIC X.
  3   FAULT-CODE       PIC X(5).
  3   FAULT-DETAILS    PIC X(20).
```

This example was carefully chosen to avoid the problem of the records being different lengths. We are now going to see how COBOL handles files in which the records are not all the same length.

COBOL can handle two types of variable length record

type 1:   different formats of record on the same file with the different formats being of different lengths — eg the above example with FAULT-DETAILS being PIC X(15)

type 2:   each record containing a table of items with a different number of items in different records — an example of this is an order record containing details of each item ordered with different orders containing different numbers of items.

We will look at each of these types of variable length record file in turn.

15.1   FILES WITH MULTIPLE RECORD TYPES

These are files with more than one type of record. In general each type of record will be a different length from the others (see figure 15.1).

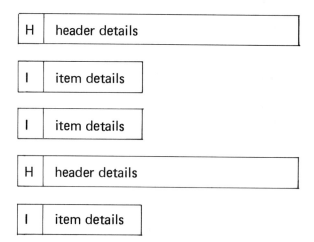

Figure 15.1 A File with Multiple Record Types of Different Length

The records are defined as usual in the File Section (see figure 15.2) and the compiler will recognise they are of different lengths.

```
FILE SECTION.
FD      ORDERS-IN . . .
1       ORDER-HEADER.
   3      REC-CODE         PIC X.
      88 HEADER-RECORD                    VALUE "H".
   3      HEADER-DETAILS PIC X(50).
1       ORDER-ITEM.
   3      REC-CODE         PIC X.
      88 ITEM-RECORD                      VALUE "I".
   3      ITEM-DETAILS     PIC X(20).
```

Figure 15.2 A File with Different Lengthed Records

When reading a file of this type you must, as with records of the same length, identify which record type you have read and then use the appropriate record description.

When writing the records, we use the normal WRITE statement:

WRITE record-name

Since in the WRITE statement we specify the record-name (rather than the file-name) the computer will know what sized record to write.

Thus everything is taken care of for you. Most compilers implement variable lengthed records by storing the length of the record in a field at the start of each record. This is automatic and should not concern the programmer.

15.2   RECORDS CONTAINING A VARIABLE NUMBER OF ITEMS

These are records containing some fixed information (HDR in figure 15.3) followed by a data item (ITEM in figure 15.3) which is repeated a variable number of times.

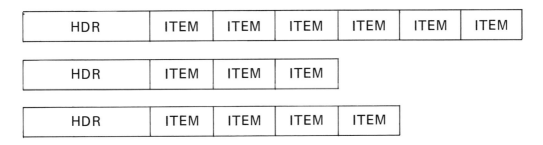

Figure 15.3   Records with a Variable Number of Items

If there is a minimum of one item and a maximum of 12 we would represent this by writing

        OCCURS 1 TO 12 TIMES

in the data description of the repeated item. When we use this variation of the OCCURS clause a method is needed to indicate the actual number of occurrences in any particular instance. To do this we use the DEPENDING ON phrase. For example in figure 15.4 the phrase

        DEPENDING ON ITEM-COUNT

is specified. This tells the computer that the actual number of occurrences (of OUT-ITEM) is stored in ITEM-COUNT. It is the programmer's responsibility to ensure that ITEM-COUNT contains the correct number. When ORDER-RECORD is written, the compiler will ensure that the specified number of OUT-ITEMs is written. Likewise if ORDER-RECORD is moved, only the specified number of OUT-ITEMs is moved. If these records are read in from a file, the programmer must check the contents of ITEM-COUNT and must only process those OUT-ITEMs that actually exist in each record.

```
        FD  ORDERS-OUT . . . .

        1    ORDER-RECORD.

            3 OUT-HEADER    PIC X(50).

            3 ITEM-COUNT    PIC 99.

            3 OUT-ITEM      PIC X(20).
                            OCCURS 1 TO 12 TIMES
                            DEPENDING ON ITEM-COUNT.
```

Figure 15.4   A Variable Length Record

In any record we can only have one data item with the OCCURS . . . DEPENDING clause. It must be the last item in the record (apart from any data items which are subordinate to it) and it must not be subordinate to a data item with an OCCURS clause. In other words we can have variable length tables but not tables of variable length items.

The two types of variable length record can be stored in the same file. In other words, in a file we may have records of several different formats some of which might contain the OCCURS DEPENDING clause.

15.3   AN EXAMPLE

The processing of both types of variable length file is demonstrated in figure 15.5. This shows a file (ORDERS-IN) consisting of header records, each of which is followed by one or more item records. The program creates a new file (ORDERS-OUT) in which all the information for each order is stored in one record: each header and all its items are stored in one record.

```
FILE SECTION.
FD    ORDERS-IN . . . .
1     ORDER-HEADER.
  3    REC-CODE        PIC X.
    88 HEADER-RECORD              VALUE "H".
  3    HEADER-DETAILS PIC X(50).
1     ORDER-ITEM.
  3    REC-CODE        PIC X.
    88 ITEM-RECORD                VALUE "I".
  3    ITEM-DETAILS    PIC X(20).
FD    ORDERS-OUT . . . .
1     ORDER-RECORD.
  3    OUT-HEADER      PIC X(50).
  3    ITEM-COUNT      PIC 99.
  3    OUT-ITEM        PIC X(20)
                       OCCURS 1 TO 12 TIMES
                       DEPENDING ON ITEM-COUNT.
WORKING-STORAGE SECTION.
1     EOF-FLAG         PIC X.
  3    END-FILE                   VALUE "Y".
PROCEDURE DIVISION.
MAIN-CONTROL.
      OPEN INPUT ORDERS-IN
           OUTPUT ORDERS-OUT
      MOVE "N" TO EOF-FLAG
      READ ORDERS-IN
        AT END MOVE "Y" TO EOF-FLAG
      END-READ
      PERFORM CREATE-ORDER UNTIL END-FILE
      CLOSE ORDERS-IN
           ORDERS-OUT
      STOP RUN.
```

(Figure 15.5 continues)

```
                        CREATE-ORDER.

                            MOVE 0 TO ITEM-COUNT

                            MOVE HEADER-DETAILS TO OUT-HEADER

                            READ ORDERS-IN

                                AT END MOVE "Y" TO EOF-FLAG

                            END-READ

                            PERFORM APPEND-ITEM

                                UNTIL END-FILE OR HEADER-RECORD

                            WRITE ORDER-RECORD.

                        APPEND-ITEM.

                            ADD 1 TO ITEM-COUNT

                            MOVE ITEM-DETAILS TO OUT-ITEM (ITEM-COUNT)

                            READ ORDERS-IN

                                AT END MOVE "Y" TO EOF-FLAG

                            END-READ.
```

Figure 15.5   Variable Length Record File Processing

15.4   SUMMARY

In this chapter we have looked at the types of variable length records permitted in COBOL:

- — multiple formats on the same file with the different formats being different lengths;

- — records which contain variable length tables specified by using the DEPENDING ON option of OCCURS.

With the latter the user must store the correct value in the DEPENDING ON data item when creating the record and must check the contents of the data item when processing the "occuring" items. In other respects the records are processed just like any other records.

QUIZ

1. How does the compiler know whether or not a file contains variable length records?

2. Which of the following record definitions are valid?

```
   (a)  1    ORDER-RECORD.

            3   CUSTOMER-NO         PIC 9(6).

            3   NAME-AND-ADD-LINE PIC X(20) OCCURS 5.

            3   NO-OF-BRANDS       PIC 99.

            3   BRAND-PURCHASED               OCCURS 1 TO 15
                                              DEPENDING ON NO-OF-BRANDS.

              5 BRAND-CODE          PIC X(5).

              5 QUALITY             PIC 999.
```

```
(b)  1   NAME-AND-ADDRESS.
     3   N-AND-A-LINE                          OCCURS 5.
     5   LINE-LENGTH          PIC 99.
     5   N-AND-A-CHARACTER    PIC X      OCCURS 1 TO 20
                                         DEPENDING ON LINE-LENGTH.


(c)  1   N-AND-A-RECORD.
     3   NAME-AND-ADD-LINES   PIC X(20) OCCURS 1 TO 5
                                         DEPENDING ON NO-OF-LINES.
     3   NO-OF-LINES          PIC 9.

(d)  1   SALES-LIST.
     3   SALESMEN-COUNT       PIC 99.
     3   SALES                PIC 9(6)  OCCURS 1 TO 100
                                         DEPENDING ON SALESMAN-COUNT.

(e)  1   ORDER-RECORD.
     3   NO-OF-BRANDS         PIC 99.
     3   BRAND-PURCHASED                 OCCURS 1 TO 15
                              DEPENDING ON NO-OF-BRANDS.
     5 BRAND-SIZE             PIC 999    OCCURS 5.
```

3. Assume the following record has just been read in and moved to ORDER-RECORD (where ORDERS-OUT is an output file).

```
FD ORDERS-OUT . . . .

     1     ORDER-RECORD.

       3   CUSTOMER-NO        PIC 9(6).

       3   NAME-AND-ADD-LINE  PIC X(20) OCCURS 5.

       3   NO-OF-BRANDS       PIC 99.

       3   BRAND-PURCHASED                OCCURS 1 TO 15.

                              DEPENDING ON NO-OF-BRANDS.

         5 BRAND-CODE         PIC X(5).

         5 QUANTITY           PIC 9(6).
```

Write the coding which will check whether there is room for one more BRAND-PURCHASED and if there is move EXTRA-BRAND into the next free position and write the record (including the extra brand) to ORDERS-OUT.

OTHER FEATURES

1. File Description Clauses

Two of the clauses in the file description (FD) entry have special formats for variable length records.

If the RECORD CONTAINS clause is used it must be of the form

RECORD CONTAINS integer-1 TO integer-2 CHARACTERS

where integer-1 is the minimum lengthed record and integer-2 is the maximum. Since the compiler can calculate these values for itself there is no need to ever use this clause.

If the BLOCK CONTAINS clause is used it would normally be in the form

BLOCK CONTAINS integer-1 TO integer-2 CHARACTERS

where integer-1 is the minimum block size and integer-2 the maximum. The method of calculating the values of integer-1 and integer-2 varies between different compilers.

2. Rewriting Variable Length Records

In Standard COBOL Indexed and Relative files may contain variable length records. The only restriction, applying to all file organisations, is that when you REWRITE a record it must be the same length as the one being overwritten.

16 Unstructured COBOL

This book has presented COBOL in a form which is in keeping with generally accepted principles of structured programming.

When used in writing new programs, the approach presented in the book will lead naturally to well structured coding. The reader might, however, face problems in the following circumstances

— when using a compiler which does not fully support ANS 8X COBOL

— when maintaining programs written in ANS 74 COBOL

If neither of these circumstances apply to you there is little point in reading this chapter. However, for those who find it relevant, this chapter covers the following topics

— procedure division sections

— conditional statements and sentences

— alternative branches (NOT AT END, etc)

16.1   PROCEDURE DIVISION SECTIONS

If desired, the Procedure Division paragraphs can be grouped into sections as follows:

```
PROCEDURE DIVISION.

Section-name SECTION.        ⎫
Paragraph                    ⎪
Paragraph                    ⎬  a section
    .                        ⎪
    .                        ⎪
    .                        ⎭

Section-name SECTION.  ⟍⟋ ── a section header
Paragraph
```

Thus the Procedure Division can be made up of a number of sections. If there are any sections the whole Division must be written in sections. Each section consists of a section-name followed by a full stop followed by any number of paragraphs. All the paragraphs up to the next section, or to the end of the program (whichever comes first) are included in the section.

The section-name is constructed according to the same rules as paragraph-names.

In ANS 74 COBOL, sections were used for two reasons:

— before the introduction of structured facilities such as END-IF and in-line PERFORM the coding tended to be broken down into much smaller paragraphs. In such circumstances it was useful to be able to group logically related paragraphs into one section. These sections could be PERFORMed (a section-name may be specified anywhere that "procedure-name" appears in a format);

— in ANS 74 COBOL SORT, an input or output procedure has to consist of one or more sections.

With ANS 8X COBOL, and its structure facilities, sections have little to offer.

16.2   CONDITIONAL STATEMENTS AND SENTENCES

In ANS 74 COBOL there are no END- scope delimiters (END-IF, END-READ, etc). All statements with conditional code such as IF, READ, and WRITE (with INVALID KEY) were known as conditional statements. Other statements were known as imperative statements. In the absence of END- scope delimiters, conditional statements were terminated with a full stop, for example

```
IF IN-STOCK-CODE NOT = STORED-STOCK-CODE
   WRITE STOCK-RECORD
   INVALID KEY PERFORM STOCK-FILE-ERROR.
```

The full stop terminates all unfinished statements: in this case the IF statement and the WRITE statement. It is equivalent in structured COBOL to

```
IF  IN-STOCK-CODE NOT = STORED-STOCK-CODE
THEN
     WRITE STOCK-RECORD
     INVALID KEY PERFORM STOCK-FILE-ERROR
     END-WRITE
END-IF
```

(Note that with ANS 74 COBOL, the noiseword THEN is not permitted although many compilers do permit it.)

A statement or string of statements terminated by a full stop is known as a sentence. A paragraph may contain any number of sentences. With structured COBOL a paragraph will always consist of precisely one sentence.

This distinction between conditional statements and imperative statements, and the use of a single all powerful scope delimiter caused many problems. These problems are avoided by always using the END- scope delimiters as demonstrated throughout this book.

However, for compatibility reasons, the old unstructured constructs are still permitted in ANS 8X COBOL and you might need to be aware of them if you debug or amend someone else's program.

16.3   ALTERNATIVE BRANCHES

In ANS 8X COBOL every statement with conditional code has an alternative branch. Thus the READ with the AT END branch also has the NOT AT END branch, for example

```
READ CUSTOMER-FILE
AT END
    MOVE HIGH-VALUE TO KEY-FILED
NOT AT END
    MOVE CUSTOMER-RECORD TO CUSTOMER-STORE
END-READ
```

Some compilers do not support the alternative branches (such as NOT AT END). This causes problems if the statement is nested in another statement (such as an EVALUATE). The simplest solution is to set a flag in the one permitted branch and use an IF statement to test it. So the above example would be coded as

```
READ CUSTOMER-FILE
AT END
    MOVE "Y" TO EOF-FLAG
END-READ
IF EOF-FLAG = "Y"
THEN
    MOVE HIGH-VALUE TO KEY-FIELD
ELSE
    MOVE CUSTOMER-RECORD TO CUSTOMER-SCORE
END-IF
```

(assuming that EOF-FLAG does not contain "Y" when execution of the READ begins).

This coding is rather cumbersome but it is well structured and can be freely nested in any other statement.

Appendix 1   Quiz Answers

CHAPTER 1

1.   IDENTIFICATION

   ENVIRONMENT

   DATA

   PROCEDURE

2.   The errors are

   (i)   PROGRAM-ID paragraph missing

   (ii)   ENVIRONMENT misspelt

   (iii)   There should not be a hyphen in CONFIGURATION SECTION

   (iv)   There should be space following the full stop after OBJECT-COMPUTER

   (v)   There should be a hyphen in SOURCE-COMPUTER

   (vi)   SOURCE-COMPUTER should come before OBJECT-COMPUTER

CHAPTER 2

1.   They are all valid except

      (b)   no letter

      (d)   £ not permitted

      (e)   = not permitted

      (h)   . not permitted

      (i)   – must not be last character

      (k)   cannot have space in the middle of a name

      (l)   BLOCK is a reserved word

2.   They are all valid except

      (b)   . must not be last character

      (d)   only one decimal point is allowed

      (e)   none of the characters T, E or N is allowed in a numeric literal

      (f)   quotation marks not allowed

      (g)   E and embedded minus not allowed

      (h)   comma not allowed

      (i)   ± not allowed (in fact there is no such character on most computers)

3.   They are all valid except

      (b)   quotation marks missing

      (e)   embedded quotation marks only permitted when they appear as a consecutive pair

      (g)   no opening quotation marks before LET. "3" is of course a valid non-numeric literal

4.   They are all valid except

      (c)   hyphen missing

5.   The reserved words are (a), (b), (c) and (g)

6.   They are all valid except

      (d)   it is not permitted to combine two formats!

CHAPTER 3

1.   Line 1+   FILE-CONTROL heading missing

      Line 2   Full stop missing from end of Select Entry

      Line 3+   DATA DIVISION heading missing

Line 5   Full stop must not appear in middle of File Description Entry

Line 6   LABEL misspelt

Line 7   Level number 1 must appear in area A

Line 8   Full stop missing from end of Data Description Entry

Line 9   PICTURE not allowed at group level

Line 12   Data name must be single word (STOCK-LEVEL would be OK)

Line 12   PICTURE missing

Line 13   REORDER is not the file-name (REORDER-FILE should have been specified)

2.   The LABEL RECORDS clause.

3.   BLOCK CONTAINS
      RECORD CONTAINS
      VALUE OF
      DATA RECORDS
      LINAGE

4.   Numbers 1 to 49 inclusive

5.   EMP-NUMBER occupies 4 characters of storage

      EMP-ADDRESS occupies 57 characters of storage

      EMPLOYEE-DETAILS occupies 96 characters of storage

6.   The record is called EMPLOYEE-DETAILS

      The group items are EMPLOYEE-DETAILS and EMP-ADDRESS

7.   Elementary items

8.   PIC 9(7).

9.   FILLER.

CHAPTER 4

1.   line 1 +   paragraph-name missing

      line 2   INPUT missing from OPEN statement

      line 3   OUTPUT missing from OPEN statement

      line 4 +   AT END phrase and END-READ missing

      line 7   File-name (STOCK-FILE-COPY) used instead of record name (whatever it is)

      line 9   STOCK-FILE-COPY is not closed

      line 10   STOP RUN should be in area B

2.   They are all valid except:

   (d)   cannot have INPUT or OUTPUT in CLOSE

   (f)   PRINT-FILE cannot be input

3.   (a)   OPEN

   (b)   READ

   (c)   WRITE

   (d)   no single verb can do this (the record would have to be read into central store and then
         written to disk)

   (e)   MOVE

   (f)   MOVE

   (g)   PERFORM

   (h)   READ (with the AT END phrase)

   (i)   CLOSE

   (j)   STOP RUN

4.   (a) – (d)   valid

   (e)   valid provided CODE-STORE contains numeric digits

   (f)   invalid

   (g)   valid (group items are regarded as alphanumeric – however you should not
                     access NUM-CODE while it has spaces in – it would probably give a run time
                     error)

   (h) & (i)   valid

5.   (a)   valid

   (b)   invalid – not unique

   (c)   valid

   (d)   invalid – not unique (also a bonus mark for spotting illegal use of reserved word DAY
         as a data-name)

   (e)   valid

   (f)   valid

   (g)   valid

   (h)   valid

CHAPTER 5

1(a) 19 characters of storage are reserved (the two record types share the same storage area)

(b) by using RECORD-CODE

(c) the first character of DB-DATE is accessed (this should never happen!)

2(a) invalid – need non-numeric literal with alphanumeric item

(b) valid

(c) invalid – SPACES is non-numeric and cannot therefore be used

(d) invalid – at a group level only non-numeric literals can be used (group items are always alphanumeric)

(e) valid

(f) valid

3.   WRITE PRINTLINE FROM REPORT-HEADING.

4.   IF RECORD-CODE = 1
       THEN
          ADD 1 TO DEBIT-COUNT
       END-IF
       ADD 1 TO RECORD-COUNT

CHAPTER 6

1.   A PERFORM statement may not (directly or indirectly) perform itself – in this case the first PERFORM performs the second PERFORM which in turn performs the first PERFORM

2.   IF QUANTITY IS NOT NUMERIC
       THEN
           PERFORM REJECT-ORDER
       END-IF

3.   (a)   2.

       (b)   5.

4.   EVALUATE TRUE
       WHEN HIGH-DISCOUNT AND BALANCE > 500
           MOVE 10 TO DISCOUNT
       WHEN HIGH-DISCOUNT AND BALANCE NOT > 500
           MOVE 5 TO DISCOUNT
       OTHERWISE
           MOVE 2 TO DISCOUNT
       END-EVALUATE

5. 3   MONTH   PIC 99.
      88   YEAR-END   VALUE 12.
      88   QUARTERLY   VALUE 1 4 7 10.
      88   SEASONAL   VALUE 5 THRU 9.
                      .
                      .

        IF YEAR--END
           PERFORM YEAR-END-PROCESS
        END-IF
        IF QUARTERLY
           PERFORM QUARTERLY-PROCESS
        END-IF
        IF SEASONAL
           PERFORM SEASONAL-PROCESS
        END-IF

6. The fact that in some cases (eg when MONTH is 4) the conditions in more than one IF statement are true. No more than one branch of EVALUATE is ever executed.

CHAPTER 7

1. (a) 99V99

    (b) V999

    (c) 999

    (d) S99

    (e) S999V99

2. After the last digit (it is the same as PICTURE 9999V).

3. (a) | 0 | 0 | 2 | 5 |

    (b) | 0 | 0 | (This MOVE is pointless)

    (c) | 1 | 0 |

    (d) | 0 | 5 | 6 | 0 |

4. The values after each statement are as follows (the values which are altered by the statement appear in bold print).

	A	B	C	D	E
(a)	2	4	**14**	20	−1
(b)	2	4	**9**	20	−1
(c)	this statement is not allowed in ANS 74 COBOL				
(d)	2	4	8	**16**	−1
(e)	2	4	8	20	**16**
(f)	2	4	8	**32**	−1
(g)	2	4	**32**	20	−1
(h)	2	4	8	**10**	−1

    (i)   this statement is not allowed in ANS 74 COBOL

(j)	2	4	**10**	20	−1
(k)	2	2	8	20	**4**

5.   COMPUTE MONTH-AVERAGE = (THIS-MONTH + LAST-MONTH) / 2

or

COMPUTE MONTH-AVERAGE = THIS-MONTH / 2 + LAST-MONTH / 2

CHAPTER 8

1.   (a) line 9

     (b) 1 blank line

     (c) line 11

2.   (a) 40 lines

     (b) line 6 of the page

     (c) line 30 of the page (line 25 of the page body)

3.   (a) `0 4 3 . 6 1`

     (b) `4 3 . 6`

     (c) Not allowed − decimal point may not be last character in picture

     (d) `0 0`

     (e) `1 0 0 4`

     (f) `0 1 6`

     (g) `1 6`

     (h) `− 1 6`

     (i) `£ 0 1 6`

     (j) `4 , 3 1 8`

     (k) `0 , 0 0 0`

     (l) `0` (note the comma is suppressed)

     (m) Not allowed − S not allowed in numeric edited pictures

4.   1   TIME-OF-DAY.

```
   3 HOUR-OF-DAY  PIC 99.
   3 REST-OF-TIME PIC 9(6).
       .
       .
       .
   ACCEPT TIME-OF-DAY FROM TIME
```

CHAPTER 9

1.   1   TV-RECORD.
        3   INTERVIEWEE   PIC X(30).
        3   PROGRAM-CHOICE   OCCURS 10 TIMES.
          5 PROGRAM-NAME   PIC X(20).
          5 POPULARITY   PIC 99.

Any names will do providing they are at least as meaningful.

2.   (a)   500.

     (b)   PRICE (15, 2).

     (c)   PRICE (1, 4) occupies characters 16, 17 and 18.

           DISCOUNT (1, 4) occupies characters 19 and 20.

           BRAND-SIZE (2, 1) occupies characters 21 to 25 inclusive.

           BRAND (20) occupies characters 381 to 400 inclusive.

3.   (a)   invalid — PRICE-LIST may not have a subscript.

     (b)   invalid — a subscript may not be subscripted.

     (c)   invalid — subscripts must follow all qualifiers.

     (d)   valid.

     (e)   invalid — the maximum permitted value of the second subscript is 4.

     (f)   invalid — subscript missing.

     (g)   invalid — cannot have arithmetic expression as a subscript. (This would be permitted if
                 SIZE-CODE was defined as an index — see later.)

4.   (a)   1   MARKER-VALUES.
             3   FILLER   PIC S9   VALUE -1.
             3   FILLER   PIC S9   VALUE -1.
             3   FILLER   PIC S9   VALUE -1.
             3   FILLER   PIC S9   VALUE -1.
             3   FILLER   PIC S9   VALUE -1.
           1   MARKER-TABLE REDEFINES MARKER-VALUES.
             3   MARKER   PIC S9   OCCURS 5.

     (b)

           1   MARKER-NO   PIC 9.
                     .
                     .
                     .

                PERFORM INITIALISE-MARKERS
                     VARYING MARKER-NO FROM 1 BY 1
                     UNTIL MARKER-NO > 5
                     .
                     .
                     .

           INITIALISE-MARKERS.
                MOVE -1 TO MARKER (MARKER-NO).

CHAPTER 10

1.   (a)   CALL "DATE–CONVERT" USING COMPACT–DATE READABLE–DATE

     (b)   LINKAGE SECTION.

          1   COMPACT–DATE.

             3   IN–YEAR   PIC 99.

             3   IN–MONTH PIC 99.

             3   IN–YEAR   PIC 99.

          1   READABLE–DATE.

             3   OUT–DAY   PIC Z9.

             3   FILLER   PIC X.

             3   OUT–MONTH PIC XXX.

             3   FILLER   PIC X.

             3   OUT–YEAR PIC 99.

     (c)   PROCEDURE DIVISION USING COMPACT–DATE READABLE–DATE.

2.   (a)   CALL

     (b)   PERFORM (with TIMES or UNTIL)

     (c)   CALL (with USING)

     (d)   CALL

CHAPTER 11

(a)   None (no CLOSE statements either)

(b)   once

(c)   In a Select entry (SELECT AMENDMENTS . . .) and a Sort Description entry (SD AMEND-MENTS . . .)

(d)   the name of the record following the SD entry for AMENDMENTS

(e)   none – RETURN can only be used in an output procedure

(f)   no

(g)

07	810415	JKL . . .
04	810416	GHI . . .
05	810416	ABC . . .
06	810417	DEF . . .
06	810417	MNO . . .

or the last two records might end up in the other order (in Standard COBOL, records with identical key values can end up in any order).

CHAPTER 12

1. ORGANIZATION IS INDEXED
    ACCESS MODE IS SEQUENTIAL (or RANDOM)
    RECORD KEY IS data-name

2. (a) The record with key value 6
    (b) It could be any record in the file

3. (a) the key value of the record being written is less than or equal to the key value of the
        last record written
    (b) there is no record with the specified key value
    (c) there is no record which matches the specified key value

CHAPTER 13

1. (a) OPEN I-O
    (b) REWRITE
    (c) DELETE
    (d) WRITE

2. The transaction file must be in the same sequence as the master file for sequential updates

3. (a) no record with the specified key value exists
    (b) no record with the specified key value exists
    (c) a record with the specified key value already exists

CHAPTER 14

1.  ```
    INSPECT INPUT-VALUE
        REPLACING LEADING SPACES BY ZEROS
    MOVE 0 TO SIGN-FLAG
    INSPECT INPUT-VALUE
        TALLYING SIGN-FLAG FOR ALL "-"
    INSPECT INPUT-VALUE
        REPLACING ALL "-" BY ZEROS
    ```

2.  ```
    MOVE SPACES TO NAME
    STRING
        SURNAME DELIMITED BY SPACE
        ", " FIRST-INITIAL "." DELIMITED BY SIZE
        INTO NAME
    ```

    Note that the MOVE is necessary to ensure that the unused characters in NAME are space filled.

3.   UNSTRING NAME
        DELIMITED BY ", " OR "."
        INTO SURNAME
              FIRST-INITIAL

General Comment: INSPECT, STRING and UNSTRING have so many options that it is nearly always possible to produce more than one solution to any problem. If you have different solutions you should check the *Reference Summary* to ensure that your solutions are equivalent to the ones given.

CHAPTER 15

1.   The compiler examines the record definitions following the file description entry. The file is a fixed length record file only if there is no occurs clause with the DEPENDING option and all record formats describe records of the same length.

2.   (a) valid

     (b) invalid — an OCCURS with the DEPENDING phrase may not be subordinate to any data item with the OCCURS clause

     (c) invalid — an item described by the OCCURS clause with the DEPENDING phrase must be the last data item in the record

     (d) invalid — the DEPENDING data item is not large enough to hold the largest occurrence number: it should have PIC 999.

     (e) valid

3.   IF   NO-OF-BRANDS < 15
     THEN
        ADD 1 TO NO-OF-BRANDS
        MOVE EXTRA-BRAND TO BRAND-PURCHASED (NO-OF-BRANDS)
        WRITE ORDER-RECORD
     END-IF

Appendix 2 ANS 8X Features Not Covered

Full ANS 8X COBOL is a very large language. There is little point in learning the whole language because some of the features are rarely used, indeed some of them are not supported by many compilers. The features omitted from this book are:

The report writer This allows the user to describe, in the Data Division, a report including detail lines, page headings and footings, and control break headings and footings. The execution of a single statement in the Procedure Division will set up and print the detail line along with any headings and footings which are appropriate. It is a valuable feature but few standard implementations are available.

The communications module This is used to send and receive messages to remote devices. It is more complicated than is necessary for most programs and many implementors have provided alternative message processing facilities.

Segmentation This is used to overlay Procedure Division sections. It is superseded on many machines by CALL/CANCEL and operating systems which support virtual storage. It is scheduled for deletion from the Standard.

Declaratives These are special routines which are executed automatically when certain exceptions occur in the Procedure Division. They can be used as an alternative to the AT END and INVALID KEY phrases used with input-output statements. They can also be used for debugging and with the report writer.

COLLATING SEQUENCE clause This is used for specifying alternatives to the native collating sequence.

CODE-SET clause This is used to write sequential files using an alternative to the native code set.

RERUN clause This is used to restart programs part way through a run after a machine failure.

SAME clause The same central storage space can be used for two or more files by the use of this clause.

MULTIPLE FILE TAPE clause This is intended for when more than one file resides on the same magnetic tape. It is scheduled for deletion from the Standard.

Unary + and -   The unary minus may be used in arithmetic expressions to negate a data item. Any arithmetic expression can be rewritten to avoid its use. The unary plus acts purely as documentation.

REVERSED option of OPEN This is used to read a sequential file in reverse order.

NO REWIND option of OPEN This may be used when a file is already positioned at its start before it is opened.

RENAMES clause This is used to give an alternative name to a group of data items in a record. The same effect can be obtained using REDEFINES.

level 77   When a level 1 data item has no subordinate data items (ie it is elementary) level number 77 may be used instead of 1. Since this achieves nothing, level 77 is due for deletion from the next standard.

ALTER statement This can be used to alter the procedure-name specified in a GO TO statement during the running of the program. It is generally considered to be very bad practice and is scheduled for deletion from the next standard. It is scheduled for deletion from the Standard.

Switch Status condition These are intended as a means of communication between the operating system (and/or the operator) and the program.

STOP literal This was intended as a means of sending messages to the operator. With the advent of more sophisticated operating systems this statement is virtually obsolete. It is scheduled for deletion from the Standard.

Nested Programs Programs can be nested inside programs (rather like Pascal Procedures) and can be executed by means of the CALL statement. Global data and files can be defined in a program and can be accessed from within the nested programs.

INITIALIZE statement This can initialize the contents of any data item (including a table) to spaces, zeros or any other specified values.

Reference Modification This permits access to any substring of characters in a data item.

REPLACE statement This permits specified pieces of source text, wherever they occur in the program, to be replaced by alternative pieces of text. It provides some of the facilities of a text editor.

De-editing Edited data items can be moved to un-edited fields.

SET condition-name TO TRUE statement A condition-name can be set to true.

Most implementations provide some additional non-standard features. No attempt has been made to cover any of these in this book.

Index

For the convenience of the reader, a combined index for this book and its companion volume — *Structured COBOL Reference Summary* — is provided. The reader is reminded that the entries for *Structured COBOL Programming* are of a conceptual and introductory nature, whilst those for the *Reference Summary* provide more complete and factual information on the individual features of COBOL.